CONTENTS

family history on the net

family history on the net

FAMILY HISTORY
ON THE

2007/8

Colin Waters

COUNTRYSIDE BOOKS

First published 2007
© Colin Waters, 2007

COUNTRYSIDE BOOKS
3 Catherine Road
Newbury, Berkshire

To view our complete range of books,
please visit us at
www.countryside www.countrysidebooks.co.uk

ISBN 978 1 84674 062 6

Designed by Peter Davies
Produced through MRM Associates Ltd., Reading
Printed by Cambridge University Press

*All material for the manufacture of this book was
sourced from sustainable forests.*

Introduction

Searching the internet is now by far the easiest and quickest way to find much of the information needed to compile a family history (though it must be remembered that to ensure accuracy, once records and information have been collected, they should wherever possible be verified using original source documents). An unimaginable amount, including family trees, census forms and other research material, both public and privately held, has been made available to genealogists on the net. Much of it would not be accessible in any other form and there is the added bonus that photographs, for instance, or family histories can be obtained by simply contacting other people researching the same subjects who have placed their contact details online. A useful feature of the internet is the ability to join a mailing list or forum, where queries, information and discussions take place on any given theme.

However, even regular users of the internet can find it is difficult to know where to start or which websites will be most useful to them on a particular subject. This book is designed to help solve these problems and to be easy to use whether you are a complete beginner in family history research or an accomplished genealogist.

In order to make using the book as easy as possible, these websites are grouped around particular subjects, in alphabetical order, and many will take you straight to the topic you are interested in. For example, if you are seeking genealogical information for any specific English county you need only look under 'England' in the *Archives, Libraries, Collections and Resources (UK)* section to find a website address that will lead to a full list of counties from which you can make your choice using a single click of the computer mouse. This saves you from having to trawl through long lists of separate printed entries and also reduces the tedious task of continually typing lengthy website addresses. To aid selection, all entries are followed by a brief summary of their content, though as some sites are very diverse in nature it will often be necessary to access a website in order to get a full picture of the exact format and type of information available. The index will also help you to find individual items or subjects throughout the book.

Care has been taken only to include sites that are of genuine use to the family historian. Those that are difficult to use or continually bombard the internet user with advertisement 'pop-ups', or even worse lock the user onto their website making it difficult to leave, have been omitted.

With literally billions of websites available, it is inevitable that not every site can be listed in a book such as this and each category can only carry a selective sample of the multitude available to the internet user. Also, because of the ever changing nature of the internet, it is not impossible that some of those listed will change or close altogether during the lifetime of this book. Nevertheless, because the same information is available from a number of sources, simply searching for a similar site under the same heading should solve the problem. Alternatively, appropriate sites can be reached by using one of the links in the first section of the book: *Comprehensive Genealogical Sites.*

With this book as your companion, you can be sure to make the best of your 'surfing' experience.

FAMILY HISTORY ON THE

THE NATIONAL ARCHIVES

Records concerning virtually every subject in this book will be found at The National Archives at Kew. In order to avoid constantly repeating the website address, the general information page and online document search page has been placed here for easy reference.

http://www.nationalarchives.gov.uk (Main website)
http://www.nationalarchives.gov.uk/documentsonline/ (Online documents search facility)

FAMILY HISTORY COURSES & TUTORIALS

If you are new to researching your family tree you should start here!

http://www.my-history.co.uk/acatalog/Genealogy_Courses.html (A selection of courses in all regions)
http://www.pharostutors.com/coursedescriptions.php#001 (About free online courses)
http://www.ihgs.ac.uk (Website of the Institute of Heraldic and Genealogical Studies, with details of courses)
http://www.doncasterfhs.co.uk/main/journal.htm (Family history tutorial for beginners)
http://www.virtualbrum.co.uk/genealogy/starting.htm (A beginner's guide to genealogy)

COMPREHENSIVE GENEALOGY SITES & SEARCH ENGINES

Rather than type in long internet addresses, it is sometimes easier to go to a particular website's homepage and to click on the resource required. Below, in alphabetical order, are listed some of the more well known sites dealing with the whole spectrum of genealogy. These can be used as an alternative means of access to many of the individual pages listed later in this book. More specialised listings will be found in the subject guide. The sites listed in this section vary in design and purpose but on the whole provide a wide range of resources for the family historian, ranging from online documents and lists of names and addresses to facilities for searching for names, dates, events or places. Many also provide research tips as well as links to other useful sites and records covering similar subjects. On the whole they are free to use, though you may have to register to get a password so as to access information. Others are partially free or only accessible by subscription. It is always worth checking whether the records you require are available free elsewhere on the internet before subscribing to pay-to-use sites.

A2A
http://www.a2a.org.uk (Database containing catalogues describing over 10 million records held locally in England and Wales dating from the 8th century to the present day)

ABIKA
http://www.abika.com/Reports/verifyemail.htm (US-based site allowing the tracing of people past and present using various resources)

ABILITY
http://www.ability.org.uk/genealogy_searchable_databases.html (Links to specific genealogy search engines and databases)

ACCESS GENEALOGY
http://www.accessgenealogy.com/ (Strongly US-biased site with links to other countries' records)

ANCESTRY
http://www.ancestry.co.uk (A selection of both free and subscription searches)
http://www.ancestry.co.uk/search/ (Search for your forebears by name, date or region)

ARCHIVES HUB
http://www.archiveshub.ac.uk/ (Search university and college archives)

AWESOME GENEALOGY
http://www.awesomegenealogy.com/ (Heavily biased to American research)

BRITISH HISTORY ONLINE
http://www.british-history.ac.uk/search.asp (Useful for historic surnames or related places and occupations as well as deeds, official records and documents of all kinds)

BRITISH ISLES GENEALOGY
http://www.bigenealogy.com/ (Specifically caters for British, Irish and Channel Islands genealogy)

BUBL
http://www.bubl.ac.uk/link/linkbrowse.cfm?menuid=11374 (Catalogue of internet family history resources)

CORAWEB
http://www.coraweb.com.au/index.htm (An Australian site with some very useful UK links)

CYNDI'S LIST
http://www.cyndislist.com/ (Considered to be one of the best free family history sites on the internet, though US-biased, Cyndi's List covers every subject imaginable concerning world-wide genealogy)

DMOZ
http://www.dmoz.org/Society/Genealogy/ (Search for any name, address, date, phrase etc on the web)

FAMILY HISTORY ONLINE
http://www.familyhistoryonline.net/ (Site run by the Federation of Family History Societies – free search but fees payable for full information)

FAMILY RECORDS UK
http://www.familyrecords.gov.uk/ (Official site with links to main records and advice)

FAMILY RELATIVES INFO
http://www.familyrelatives.info/#free (Extremely useful listing of all free family history resources on the web together with pay-to-view records)

FAMILY SEARCH
http://www.familysearch.org (Search what is claimed to be the largest collection of free genealogy records in the world, provided by the LDS (Mormon) Church, including the IGI and 1881 census)

FAMILY TREE SEARCHER
http://www.familytreesearcher.com/ (Searches multiple sites and gives tips on research)

FIND MY PAST
http://www.findmypast.com (Lots of resources – pay to view individual records or subscribe to view all)

FREE-UK-GEN
http://freeukgen.rootsweb.com/ (A continuously expanding free resource for birth, marriage and death, census and other records)

GENEALOGIST
http://www.thegenealogist.co.uk/ (Pay-to-view genealogy site with lots of records. Has a UK bias)

GENEALOGY LINKS UK
http://www.genealogy-links.co.uk/ (UK genealogy links including those to specific counties)

GENEALOGY LINKS.NET
http://www.genealogylinks.net/ (Thousands of links to worldwide genealogy resources)

GENEALOGY RESOURCES
http://www.50connect.co.uk/50c/genealogylibrary.asp (A wide range of links useful to genealogists)

GENEALOGY TODAY
http://www.genealogytoday.com/uk/ (Selection of both free and fee-based UK genealogy resources and searches)

GENEAT
http://www.geneanet.org/premiers_pas/archives.php (Allows you to search submitted family history files and includes a message board)

GENES REUNITED
http://www.genesreunited.co.uk/ (Commercial site with many resources; search births, marriages and deaths and censuses using 300 million official records, plus contact facilities)

GENGATEWAY
http://www.gengateway.com/ (Gateways, links and guides to a vast array of genealogical information)

GENSOURCE
http://www.gensource.com/ (Worldwide genealogy with a link to British sources)

GENUKI
http://www.genuki.org.uk/ (The main page of this resourceful UK and Ireland genealogy website with an ever-growing database of information and contacts; it offers a vast range of very useful free information and guides)

GENWEB
http://www.britishislesgenweb.org/ (British Isles genealogy with links to Genweb sites in other countries)

GIC (GLOBAL INFORMATION CENTRE)
http://www.gic.co.uk/roots.htm (Miscellaneous family history website links)

GOOGLE GENEALOGY
http://www.genealogy-search-help.com/ (A special search site for genealogists using Google, one of the most widely used search engines on the net)

GRI (GENEALOGY RESOURCES ON THE INTERNET)
http://www-personal.umich.edu/~cgaunt/gen_web.html (World genealogy site index)
http://www-personal.umich.edu/~cgaunt/uk.html (UK section of the same site)

HEARTLAND
http://www.geocities.com/Heartland/6266/indexes.htm (Links to various family tree resources)

IRELAND GENEALOGY PROJECTS
http://irelandgenealogyprojects.rootsweb.com/ (Gateway linked to Irish genealogy)

LOOKIN 4 KIN
http://www.looking4kin.com/ (Genealogical resources and chatroom)

LOOKUP UK.COM
http://www.uklookups.com/ (US based site with a variety of UK genealogical resources and surname search)

MENAI
http://www.menai.ac.uk/read/search_tools_more.asp (A good choice here of search engines available on the internet)

OGRE
http://www.cefnpennar.com/index.htm (Name search with links to other useful family history resources)

ONE GREAT FAMILY
http://www.onegreatfamily.com/Home.aspx (General family history resources including photos, biographies and browsing by alphabet; free search but fees payable for other resources)

ORIGINS NETWORK
http://www.originsnetwork.com/ (British and Irish genealogy resources with photos – membership required)

OZEMAIL
http://members.ozemail.com.au/~clday/misc.htm (Lots of links and resources concerning the British in colonial India)

PEDIGREES & PEOPLE
http://web.ukonline.co.uk/sheila.jones/ (Gateway to lots of British resources)

ROOTSWEB
http://www.rootsweb.com/ (Many facts and resources including records and actual family trees; has a strong US bias but also caters for British genealogists)
http://worldconnect.rootsweb.com/ (A Rootsweb project to connect family historians using Gedcom files – search what's available here)
http://resources.rootsweb.com/cgi-bin/metasearch (Searches using multiple search engines)

SILVER SURFERS
http://www.silversurfers.net/findit-people.html (Designed for the older user but

provides everyone with a variety of resources and links to assist in finding people living or dead)

SOCIETY OF GENEALOGISTS
http://www.sog.org.uk/library/intro.shtml (Genealogy resources from the respected Society of Genealogists)
http://www.sog.org.uk/library/libindex.shtml (A guide to the family history records and resources held by the Society)

SURNAME NAVIGATOR
http://www.surnamenavigator.org/ (Search for a surname using a dozen or so major search engines at once)

YAHOO GENEALOGY
http://dir.yahoo.com/Arts/Humanities/History/Genealogy/ (Specialist genealogy search page on one of the oldest and most well used search engines on the net)

ALPHABETICAL SUBJECT GUIDE

ADOPTION

Official adoption only began in Britain on 1 January 1927. Before that time illegitimate, orphaned or otherwise homeless children were given up to childless families or were brought up by grandparents as the pretended sibling or cousin of their own actual parent. As a result tracing these family connections can often prove a difficult task.

http://www.familyrecords.gov.uk/topics/adoption_1.htm (Official site for accessing adoption records in England, Wales, Ireland and Scotland)

http://www.gro-scotland.gov.uk/regscot/adoption.html (Official Scottish government site for all matters regarding adoption)

http://www.nas.gov.uk/guides/adoptions.asp (Adoption records in the Scottish National Archives)

http://www.baaf.org.uk/info/bap1969.shtml (British Adoption Project 1965-1969)

http://www.afteradoption.org.uk (Advice on how to trace birth parents)

http://www.lookupuk.com/main.html (Site providing assistance to find adoption records, past and present)

http://adoptionrecords.org/ (Adoption Search website with adoption records database, links and message board)

http://www.ffhs.org.uk/General/Help/Adopted.htm (UK web page giving advice on finding or researching adopted ancestors)

http://www.adoptionsearchreunion.org.uk/default.htm (Adoption Search Reunion website)

http://www.westminster.gov.uk/healthandsocialcare/familycare/adoption/birth_records_counselling.cfm (The City of Westminster hold the adoption records of the defunct National Children Adoption Association (NCAA))

http://www.ffhs.org.uk/General/Help/Adopted.htm (FFHS site regarding tracing the birth parents of adopted persons in England and Wales)

ARCHIVES, LIBRARIES, COLLECTIONS & RESOURCES (UK & IRELAND)

The internet provides access to a variety of resources ranging from national and regional archives to collections held by organisations, businesses and individuals. The following entries list various UK and Irish resources by location and include a selection of websites found under subject headings. If your own area is not listed specifically, it can generally be found by typing the area or county name followed by the word 'records' into any internet search engine.

Archives, Libraries, Collections & Resources (UK & Ireland)

GENERAL COLLECTIONS

http://www.nationalarchives.gov.uk/ (Full guide and links to The National Archives)

http://www.nationalarchives.gov.uk/archon/ (TNA directory of national and local archives, plus overseas collections)

http://www.nationalarchives.gov.uk/search/quick_search.aspx (Search The National Archives)

http://www.york.ac.uk/inst/bihr/ (Website of the Borthwick Institute, York, which holds one of the biggest archive repositories outside London)

http://www.gmcro.co.uk/ftpfiles/carn.pdf (About CARN, the *County Archive Research Network,* and how to obtain a research ticket)

http://www.genuki.org.uk/search/ (Type the word 'archive' into Genuki's own search engine to obtain links to thousands of national and regional archive sources)

http://www.sog.org.uk/library/upper.shtml (Society of Genealogists' resources by subject)

http://earlymodernweb.org.uk/emr/ (Links to early modern sources in history including genealogy)

http://www.archiveshub.ac.uk/ (Search for university and college archives)

http://www.genealogy-links.co.uk/ (General links including those to specific counties)

http://www.ukgenweb.com/ (Contains links to regional and other family history sites in the UK)

http://www.familia.org.uk/ (UK and Ireland guide to genealogical resources in public libraries)

http://copac.ac.uk/ (Access to online catalogues of major universities and national libraries in the UK and Ireland)

http://ds.dial.pipex.com/town/square/ac940/weblibs.html (Complete list of British libraries with contact details and catalogues of resources available to the researcher)

http://www.bl.uk/ (Facilities to search the British Library for genealogy items)

http://www.york.ac.uk/inst/bihr/Links.htm (List of online archive lists and catalogues)

http://www.history.ac.uk/gh/lfguide.htm (List of guides to records held at the Guildhall Library)

http://www.genogold.com/html/news.html (Genogold site of UK genealogical resources)

http://www.curiousfox.org.uk/uk/ (Village by village genealogical queries and answers)

http://www.everygeneration.co.uk/ (Genealogy and history links for black family history in Britain)

ENGLAND

http://www.genuki.org.uk/big/eng/ (Start your search here for family tree resources for any English county)

http://www.familyrecords.gov.uk/ (Official site assisting researchers to find the family history records they need, with links)

http://www.ancestorspy.com/England/england.htm (English genealogy by county with other links)

http://www.genealogylinks.net/uk/england/ (Thousands of links specifically geared to English family history research)

http://genealogy.about.com/od/england/index.htm (Lots of English genealogy resources)

http://wilson.lib.umn.edu/reference/eng-gene.html (English and English-American genealogy)

http://www.cousinconnect.com/p/a/0/s/ENGLISH (English genealogical postings, queries and contacts)

http://www.oz.net/~markhow/englishros.htm (Alphabetical list of English record offices and archives)

http://www.cityoflondon.gov.uk/Corporation/leisure_heritage/libraries_archives_ museums_galleries/lma/lma.htm (London Metropolitan Archives)

http://www.westminster.gov.uk/archives/ (City of Westminster archives)

http://www.gunnerside.info/index.html (Extensive genealogical and other information for the areas of Gunnerside and Swaledale, North Yorkshire)

http://www.victorianlondon.org/ (Research Victorian London by subject)

http://freepages.genealogy.rootsweb.com/~liverpool/main.html (Historic Liverpool resources)

http://www.lostcousins.com/ (Links researchers looking for the same relative using the 1881 census)

http://www.berksfhs.org.uk/weblinks.htm (Berkshire Family History Society's links to general family history resources on the internet)

http://edenlinks.rootsweb.com/1gp/RECORDS/TRANSINDEX.HTM (Cumbrian genealogy resources)

http://www.whitbyarchives.org.uk/ (Yorkshire and general resources with historic pictures of the region)

WALES & ANGLESEY

http://www.genuki.org.uk/big/wal/ (Start your search here for Welsh genealogy resources)

http://www.oz.net/~markhow/welshros.htm (Alphabetical list of Welsh record offices and archives)

http://www.archivesnetworkwales.info/ (Welsh archives network with lots of links and resources)

http://www.genuki.org.uk/Societies/Wales.html (Genuki's list of Welsh Family History Societies)

http://www.censusfinder.com/wales.htm (Comprehensive list of online census material for Wales and Anglesey)

http://www.gtj.org.uk/search/searchRepository.php?lang=en&r=100 (Anglesey record office site with documents that can be read online)

http://www.cefnpennar.com/ang1873land/index.htm (Online lists of landowners in Anglesey in 1873)

http://www.curiousfox.com/history_Wales/anglesey.lasso (Village by village family

history notes, queries and postings for Anglesey)
http://www.genuki.org.uk/big/wal/CAE/Llandegai/Llandegai51.html (Complete transcription of 1851 census – Llandegai, Wales)
http://home.clara.net/tirbach/hicks3a.html#graveyard (Help in searching Welsh resources with tips for all genealogists)
http://www.welshmariners.org.uk/ (Database of thousands of Welsh mariners)
http://www.cefnpennar.com/church_list.htm (Welsh headstone and memorial inscription project)
http://www.theshipslist.com/pictures/welsh1.htm (Details about Welsh emigrants to Patagonia)

SCOTLAND

http://www.genuki.org.uk/big/sct/ (Start your search here for Scottish genealogy links)
http://www.scotlandspeople.gov.uk/content/help/index.aspx?r=1229 (Official Scottish genealogy site with links to birth, marriage and death records, census and other information)
http://www.oz.net/~markhow/scotsros.htm (Alphabetical list of Scottish Record Offices and Archives)
http://www.scan.org.uk/ (Scottish Archive network site)
http://www.gro-scotland.gov.uk/site-map.html (Scottish General Register Office site)
http://www.nas.gov.uk/ (National Archives of Scotland)
http://www.geo.ed.ac.uk/home/scotland/genealogy.html (Site specifically aimed at researching Scottish roots)
http://www.bbc.co.uk/scotland/history/scottishroots/ (BBC site with hints on how to start and continue your search for Scottish ancestors)
http://www.genuki.org.uk/Societies/Scotland.html (Genuki's list of Scottish Family History Societies)
http://www.scottishdocuments.com/wills.asp (Scottish digitisation project for wills and other historic documents)
http://www.nas.gov.uk/guides/inheriting.asp (An explanation of inheritance laws and procedures in Scotland)
http://www.bigenealogy.com/location/scotland.htm (Scotland's history and genealogy resources)
http://www.ancestralscotland.com/ (Ancestral Scotland site with genealogy search facilities)
http://www.scotsfamily.com/ (Scottish family history research facilities including photos, maps and clan information)
http://www.ancestor.abel.co.uk/links.html#pro (Miscellaneous Scottish family history links)
http://www.nas.gov.uk/guides/sheriffCourt.asp (Guide to Scottish Sheriff Court records)
http://www.fifefhs.org/Records/recordsindex.htm (Index to online records of Fife district)

http://www.electricscotland.com/argentina/index.htm (Scottish settlers in South America)
http://myweb.tiscali.co.uk/scotsinargpat/ (Scots in Argentina and Chile)
http://www.scotsgenealogy.com/online/early_scots_at_montreal.htm (Early Scots in Montreal)
http://www.abdn.ac.uk/emigration/user-guide.html (Database of Scottish emigrants)
http://www.cefnpennar.com/ebay/scottish_landowners.htm (Scottish landowners returns 1873)
http://www.gengateway.com/index.cfm?GID=22 (Links to various documents including clans of Scotland)
http://www.clansearch.co.uk/Clan%20Index.htm (Search for a clan by name)

IRELAND (including NORTHERN IRELAND)

http://www.genuki.org.uk/big/irl/ (Start your search here for family history information related to any Irish county)
http://www.irishroots.com/research.php (Search for Irish surnames, distribution etc)
http://www.proni.gov.uk/exhibiti/ontherec/genealog.htm   (Northern Ireland Public Record Office site)
ttp://www.groni.gov.uk/index.htm (Northern Ireland General Register Office site with links to researching historical records)
http://www.genealogylinks.net/uk/ireland/index.html (Irish genealogical links and resources)
http://irelandgenealogyprojects.rootsweb.com/ (Hundreds of links and resources for Ireland)
http://www.goireland.com/genealogy/ (Page with separate links to other Irish resources by category)
http://genforum.genealogy.com/ireland/ (Irish genealogy forum)
http://www.ulsterancestry.com/ua-free-pages.php (Ulster free genealogy resources)
http://www.nationalarchives.ie/ (Site of The National Archives of Ireland)
http://www.originsnetwork.com/help/helpio-census1841.aspx (Irish strays 1841 census)
http://www.ancestryireland.com/database.php (Sample data from various records, documents and lists relating to Ireland – membership scheme for full access)
http://www.censusfinder.com/irish_surnames.htm (Irish clan and surname resources)
http://www.proni.gov.uk/freeholders/intro.asp (Irish freeholder records with search facilities)
http://www.proni.gov.uk/school/explain.htm (Aids to tracing schools in Northern Ireland)
http://en.wikipedia.org/wiki/Plantations_of_Ireland (Background to 16th and 17th century settlement of the English and Scots in Ireland)
http://www.genuki.org.uk/Societies/Ireland.html (Genuki's list of Irish Family History Societies
http://www.ancestryireland.com/ (Ancestry Ireland website with ancestor search)

http://freespace.virgin.net/alan.tupman/sites/irish.htm (Lots of links to Irish passenger list sources)

http://www.cefnpennar.com/ebay/irish_landowners.htm (Irish landowner returns 1873)

http://www.accessgenealogy.com/country/ireland.htm (More Irish resources)

http://www.finditireland.com/links/irishclansites.html (Links to individual Irish clan name sites)

http://en.wikipedia.org/wiki/Williamite_war_in_Ireland (Williamite-Jacobite War in Ireland)

http://www.rootsweb.com/~irlkik/ksurnam2.htm (County Kilkenny surname list)

ISLE OF MAN

http://www.genuki.org.uk/big/iom/ (Start here when looking for IOM family history resources)

http://www.genuki.org.uk/Societies/IsleOfMan.html (Genuki's list of Isle of Man Family History Societies)

http://www.isle-of-man.com/interests/genealogy/sources.htm (Sources for IOM family history information)

http://www.genealogylinks.net/uk/england/isle-of-man/index.html (Lots of IOM genealogy links)

http://www.lawsons.ca/marriages/_mar_index.html (IOM marriages by alphabetical list)

http://www.isle-of-man.com/manxnotebook/famhist/genealgy/chomes.htm (IOM children's homes)

http://www.bigenealogy.com/location/man.htm (IOM history and genealogy)

http://www.isle-of-man.com/manxnotebook/famhist/fhsjv12.htm (Index to Manx family history journal that can be read on your computer)

http://www.isle-of-man.com/manxnotebook/famhist/pregs/lnbu1718.htm (Isle of Man burials 1718-1793)

http://www.isleofman.com/Home/Arts/Humanities/History/Genealogy/NAMA.aspx (US site with Isle of Man genealogy interests.)

http://www.isle-of-man.com/manxnotebook/famhist/genealgy/intern.htm (POW camps on the Isle of Man)

ISLES OF SCILLY

http://www.genuki.org.uk/big/eng/Cornwall/IslesofScilly/index.html (Lots of Scilly Isles genealogy links)

http://www.comp.utas.edu.au/users/rsmith/scilly/ (Scillonian site with genealogy links to information about individual families)

CHANNEL ISLANDS

http://user.itl.net/~glen/genukici.html (Start your search here for Channel Islands genealogy, island by island) http://www.genuki.org.uk/Societies/ChannelIslands.html (Genuki's list of Channel Islands Family History Societies)

ARCHIVES, LIBRARIES, COLLECTIONS & RESOURCES (OVERSEAS)

Those who have ancestors that came from or went to other countries can gain access to a wide range of records on the internet. Below are some of the main websites. Other countries may be searched for using search engines such as Google, Yahoo etc or by using the World Gen website listed below.

ALL COUNTRIES

http://www.bisa.btinternet.co.uk/layout.htm (List of countries included in the World Gen genealogical project with links to specific sites)
http://freepages.genealogy.rootsweb.com/~northing/ethnic/index.html (Links to ethnic resources on the net)
http://www.afhs.ab.ca/aids/geographic/geog.html (Links to family history sources by country or region)

AFRICA

http://www.bl.uk/collections/african.html (African records held at the British Library)
http://www.exploregenealogy.co.uk/USAfricanAmericanRecords.html (African-American genealogy)
http://www.everygeneration.co.uk/ (Motherland web page searching for black origins, with links)

AUSTRALIA

http://www.naa.gov.au/the_collection/the_collection.html (National Archives of Australia)
http://www.nla.gov.au/oz/genelist.html (Links to lots of Australian family history sites including official government resources)
http://www.bl.uk/collections/oesoz.html (Australian records held by the British Library)
http://www.records.nsw.gov.au/archives/archives_in_brief_542.asp (Leaflets, links and more concerning New South Wales government archives and records)
http://www.winthrop.dk/wc_toc.htm (Family tree of Captain Cook)

AUSTRIA

http://www.aafhg.org.uk/ (Anglo-Austrian Family History Group)

BASQUE REGIONS

http://home.earthlink.net/~fybarra/ (Basque genealogy home page)

http://www.basquemuseum.com/ (Basque Museum in USA with information, resources and links about Basque culture and history)

http://meilleursprenoms.com/site/regionaux/Basques/Basques.htm (Alphabetical list of Basque names)

BELGIUM – also WALLOON & FLEMISH ANCESTRY

http://www.genealogylinks.net/europe/belgium/index.html (Links for tracing Belgian ancestry)

http://users.pandora.be/hugo.harth/Genealogie/genbel.html (Wide range of resources and helpful links)

http://www.wallonie.com/wallang/ (Walloon language website)

http://olivetreegenealogy.com/hug/overview.shtml (Huguenot and Walloon ancestry)

http://www.genealogy-quest.com/collections/walloons.html (Walloon and French immigrants to Virginia 1621)

CANADA

http://www.collectionscanada.ca/ (National Archives of Canada)

http://www.accessgenealogy.com/country/canada.htm (Lots of Canadian resources)

http://www.accessgenealogy.com/test/canada.cgi (Canadian surname search)

http://www.rootsweb.com/~canmil/index.html (Canadian military history project)

http://www.bifhsgo.ca/ (Canadian site related to British Isles family history)

http://www.lostcousins.com/ (Links researchers looking for the same relative using the Canada 1881 census)

http://www.scotsgenealogy.com/online/early_scots_at_montreal.htm (Early Scots in Montreal)

http://www.ainc-inac.gc.ca/pr/trts/hti/Marit/bris_e.html (Background to the British administration in Nova Scotia: 1714-1739)

http://www.ubishops.ca/geoh/settlem/phases.htm (British settlement in the Eastern Townships 1820 to 1850, plus American and French settlers)

CARIBBEAN

http://www.movinghere.org.uk/galleries/roots/caribbean/occupations/occupations.htm (Information with links concerning recruitment of Caribbean men to UK, civil service posts, Merchant navy recruits and military enlistment)

http://www.everygeneration.co.uk/ (Motherland web page searching for black origins, with links)

CHINA

http://www.rootsweb.com/~chnwgw/ (Chinese genealogy resources with listings by province)
http://www.ziplink.net/~rey/ch/queries/ (Bulletin board for Chinese surname queries)
http://mail.bris.ac.uk/%7Ehirab/smp2.html (A website researching British members of the Shanghai Municipal Police 1854-1943)

CROATIA

http://www.croatia-in-english.com/ (Genealogy and other links in English specifically regarding Croatia)
http://www.croatians.com/pioneer_list.htm (Croatian pioneers in America)

CUBA

http://www.cubagenweb.org/links.htm (Cuban genealogy links)

DENMARK

http://www3.sympatico.ca/colin.swift/danish.htm (Danish / English genealogy dictionary)
http://www3.sympatico.ca/colin.swift/extr-rec.htm (Danish online family history resources)
http://members.ozemail.com.au/~clday/danish.htm (Danish family history connections in India)
http://users.rootsweb.com/~indwgw/serampore.htm (List of Danes in Serampore near Calcutta, India in 1813)

FINLAND

http://www.genealogia.fi/indexe.htm (Site of the Finnish genealogical society)
http://www.rootsweb.com/~finwgw/ (Resources for tracing your Finnish ancestors)

FRANCE

http://www.genealogylinks.net/europe/france/index.html (French genealogy resources)
http://www.theshipslist.com/ships/passengerlists/french_occupations1873.html (Old French occupations)
http://membres.geneaguide.com/affhs/AS-AFFHS.HTM (Resources from the Anglo-French Family History Society)
http://www.genealogy-quest.com/collections/walloons.html (Walloons and French who emigrated to Virginia 1621)

GERMANY

http://german.about.com/library/weekly/aa020830a.htm (Links, tips and resources for researching German ancestors)
http://www.agfhs.org.uk/ (Anglo-German Family History Society)
http://homepages.rootsweb.com/~george/oldgermanprofessions.html (German occupations)
http://www.feefhs.org/uk/indexger.html (German genealogy links)
http://home.att.net/~wee-monster/ (German genealogy links with an American perspective)
http://www.feldgrau.com/wsskb.html (German photographers in WWII)

GIBRALTAR

http://www.interment.net/data/gib/trafalgar/index.htm (Names of people buried in Gibraltar 1798-1814)

HUNGARY

http://user.itl.net/~glen/FamilyHistoryinHungary.html (Family history in Hungary; also includes Slovakia)
http://www.mol.gov.hu/?akt_menu=574&set_lang=466 (Website of National Archives of Hungary in English)

INDIA

http://www.bl.uk/collections/oiocfamilyhistory/family.html (British Library holdings for India and South Asia from the 17th century to the 20th century)
http://members.ozemail.com.au/~clday/ (Resources for researching family history in India)
http://www.sumgenius.com.au/ (Australian site with Anglo-Indian family trees and other family details)
http://members.ozemail.com.au/~clday/misc.htm (Tracking civilians in colonial India with lots of family history links)
http://users.rootsweb.com/~indwgw/Bengal/Bengal_Marriage.htm (Marriages of Europeans in Bengal, 1855-1896)
http://users.rootsweb.com/~indwgw/Bengal/Calcuttagroom.htm (Marriages of Europeans in Calcutta, 1713 – 1800)
http://members.ozemail.com.au/~clday/cem.htm (European cemeteries in India)
http://www.aigs.org.au/britind.htm (A background to British India with links)
http://www.anglo-indians.com/index.asp (The Anglo-Indian website)
http://members.ozemail.com.au/~clday/churches.htm (Church records in Colonial India)
http://www.bl.uk/collections/iorgenrl.html (How to access the records of the East India Company and related documentation)

http://www.aigs.org.au/britind.htm (Information and links about the East India Company)
http://youroldbooksandmaps.co.uk/East-India-Registers-p-1-c-52.html (Commercial site selling lists pertaining to the East India Company)

ITALY

http://italiangenealogy.tardio.com/ (Resources for tracing Italian ancestors)
http://www.anglo-italianfhs.org.uk/ (Anglo-Italian Family History Society)
http://www.geocities.com/heartland/pointe/8783/italjobs.html (Translation of Italian occupations)

JAPAN

http://www.samurai-archives.com/ (Samurai archives with genealogy link)
http://www.samurai-archives.com/clanindex.html (Clan family trees of Japanese families)

MALTA

http://www.maltafamilyhistory.com/ (Malta family history connections, mainly for British forces families)

MIDDLE EAST

http://www.rootsweb.com/~mdeastgw/ (Middle East Genweb project)

NEW ZEALAND

http://homepages.ihug.co.nz/~tonyf/ (Website dedicated to pioneers and early settlers in New Zealand)
http://www.bl.uk/collections/oesoz.html (New Zealand records held by the British Library)
http://www.wartimesindex.co.uk/infopage.php?menu=wars&display=NewZealand (Background to British involvement in the Maori wars 1844-1865)
http://freepages.genealogy.rootsweb.com/~ourstuff/ (A strange but very useful list of variable resources for New Zealand, including barmaid registrations!)
http://www.kaelewis.com/goldminers/searchpage.htm (Search for an ancestor amongst New Zealand gold miners, 1868)
http://www.angelfire.com/az/nzgenweb/links.html (Lots of New Zealand genealogy links with some area-specific ones)
http://homepages.ihug.co.nz/~origins/nzgene.htm (More useful NZ genealogy links)

NORWAY

http://www-personal.umich.edu/~cgaunt/norway.html (Resources for tracing Norwegian ancestors)
http://homepages.rootsweb.com/~norway/index.html (More Norwegian resources and links)
http://www.accessgenealogy.com/country/norway.htm (Lots of links to Norwegian records)
http://www.geocities.com/Heartland/Estates/5536/index.html (Norwegian surname database)

PORTUGAL

http://www.geocities.com/fcandido2001/portgen/general.html (Resources for Portuguese genealogy)
http://www.portugueseancestry.com/ (Search for a Portuguese ancestor with links to family trees)
http://users.rootsweb.com/~indwgw/lisbon.htm (British baptisms Lisbon, 1721-1807)

RUSSIA

http://www.genealogylinks.net/europe/russia/index.html (Lots of Russian genealogy resources including census links)
http://www.mtu-net.ru/rrr/ (How to research Russian roots plus genealogy links)
http://www.ancestry.com/search/locality/dbpage.aspx?tp=3258&p=5189 (Russian resources at Ancestry.com)

SCANDINAVIAN (All Scandinavian countries)

http://www-personal.umich.edu/~cgaunt/scandinavia.html (Resources for genealogists with Scandinavian roots)

SINGAPORE & MALAYA

http://user.itl.net/~glen/BritishinSingapore%26Malaya.html (Guide to the region with history timeline and brief description of cemetery)
http://user.itl.net/~glen/CivilianInternees.html (Civilian internees under the Japanese during World War II)
http://user.itl.net/~glen/asianintro.html (Prisoners of war and civilian prisoners in Asia with links)

SOUTH AFRICA

http://sa-passenger-list.za.net/index.php (Useful links and resources if your ancestors emigrated to South Africa)

http://www.1820settlers.com/ (A free website dedicated to the British settlers in South Africa in 1820, their descendants and researchers)
http://www.british-genealogy.com/resources/county/ntt/emigration/southafrica-1820/nttsa.htm (Nottingham settlers in South Africa 1820)
http://www.shelaghspencer.co.za/ (British settlers in Natal 1824-1857)
http://search.freefind.com/find.html?id=91621572&map=0&page=0&ics=1 (Resources and links for Victorian British settlers in Natal)

SOUTH AMERICA

http://www.british-genealogy.com/resources/county/ntt/emigration/southafrica-1820/nttsa.htm (British settlers in South America database)
http://www.bisa.btinternet.co.uk/layout.htm ('Brits in South America' database)
http://homepage.ntlworld.com/jnth/ (British settlers in Argentina with name search)
http://www.theshipslist.com/pictures/welsh1.htm (Details about Welsh emigrants to Patagonia)
http://archiver.rootsweb.com/th/read/SOUTH-AM-EMI/2004-04/1081269374 (South America genealogy message board)
http://www.electricscotland.com/argentina/index.htm (Scottish settlers in South America)
http://myweb.tiscali.co.uk/scotsinargpat/ (Scots in Argentina and Chile)

SPAIN

http://www.kindredtrails.com/spain.html (Links, tips and resources for tracing Spanish ancestors)
http://www.majercin.com/spanlinks.html (More Spanish family history resources)

SRI LANKA

http://www.rootsweb.com/~lkawgw/ (Sri Lankan genealogy website)

SWEDEN

http://www-personal.umich.edu/~cgaunt/swede.html (Resources for tracing Swedish ancestors)
http://genforum.genealogy.com/sweden/ (Swedish genealogy forum)
http://explorenorth.com/gen-swe.html (More resources for tracing your Swedish ancestry)

UNITED STATES OF AMERICA

http://geneasearch.com/cemeteries.htm (Trace ancestors buried in cemeteries in the USA)

http://www.rootsweb.com/~bifhsusa/ (USA site dedicated to British Isles Family History)
http://www.isleofman.com/Home/Arts/Humanities/History/Genealogy/NAMA.aspx (USA-Isle of Man genealogy)
http://www.lostcousins.com/ (Links researchers looking for the same relative using the US 1880 census)
http://www.accessgenealogy.com/native/index.htm (Native American Indian tribe links)
http://www.snowcrest.net/siskiyoulibrary/gold/minefram.html (Gold mine database with names of mine owners)
http://www.usgennet.org/usa/az/state/pioneers_of_tonto_basin.htm (Pioneers list of Tonto Basin, 1800s-1900s)
http://skyways.lib.ks.us/kansas/genweb/pioneers/index.html (Kansas pioneers lists)
http://www.rootsweb.com/~mopionee/ (Early Missouri settlers)
http://www.rootsweb.com/~iashelby/pioneer.htm (Shelby County, Iowa early settlers)
http://www.cagenweb.com/cpl/ (Californian Pioneer Project web page)
http://ftp.rootsweb.com/pub/usgenweb/co/yuma/history/ycpioneers.txt (Pioneers list Yuma County, Colorado)
http://www.croatians.com/pioneer_list.htm (Croatian pioneers in America)
http://www.stjosephmuseum.org/Pioneers/pioneers.htm (List of US pioneers, alphabetically arranged)

BIBLES, FAMILY

Contrary to popular opinion the interest in family history is not a modern phenomenon and in the past some families would note births, marriages and deaths in their family bible. Many have been lost but there are now both individuals and groups of people intent on preserving the records that remain.

http://www.4qd.org/BFB/Bibles/Names.html (List of British family names found in bibles)
http://www.cyndislist.com/bibles.htm (Cyndi's List index to general bible resources)
http://www.geocities.com/Heartland/Fields/2403/ (Bible Archives list of 'lost and found' family bibles)
http://www.ancestorhunt.com/family_bible_records.htm (Genealogy details extracted from family bibles)
http://www.ancestorhunt.com/family_bibles_index.htm (Search for names found in family bibles)
http://www.rootsweb.com/%7Eusgenweb/ga/gabibles.htm (US-based family bible site)
http://www.rootsweb.com/%7Emeandrhs/taylor/bible/maine.html (The Maine Family Bible Archives, USA)
http://www.complete-bible-genealogy.com/ (Genealogy of Biblical characters after whom your ancestor may have been named)

BIRTHS, MARRIAGES & DEATHS

Literally thousands of sites deal with these vital subjects and the associated subjects of baptism and burial. Most have links to each other and many can be found using the *Comprehensive Genealogy Sites* in the first section of this book. Below is a selection of general resources, together with some of the most useful web sites in particular categories. In the listings there are also some obituary links. Most modern major newspapers now have internet-based obituary pages. To find them simply type the name of the newspaper into a search engine, followed by the word 'obituaries'.

BIRTHS, MARRIAGES & DEATHS

http://www.familyrecords.gov.uk (Official site with links to The National Archives and the General Register Office (GRO))

http://www.genuki.org.uk/big/eng/CivilRegistration.html (Links and resources for civil registration in the UK and Ireland)

http://www.ukbmd.org.uk/genuki/reg/ (List of registration districts for England and Wales)

http://www.gro.gov.uk/gro/content/ (Information on how to obtain certificates)

http://www.freebmd.org.uk/ (Free search through GRO birth, marriage and death indexes; check years available)

http://www.1901censusonline.com/bmd.asp?wci=BMDlanding&searchtype=10 (Search birth, marriage and death GRO indexes 1837-2004 for England and Wales)

http://homepage.ntlworld.com/hitch/gendocs/info_bmd.html (Guide to birth, marriage and death certificates available from the General Register Office for England and Wales)

http://www.familysearch.org/Eng/Search/frameset_search.asp (Gives free access to the LDS (Mormon) Church's vast family history collection of records of all religions, including the International Genealogical Index)

http://freepages.genealogy.rootsweb.com/~hughwallis/IGIBatchNumbers.htm (How to search the IGI (above) using batch numbers)

http://www.ukbdm.co.uk/ (UK site for exchanging details from birth, marriage and death certificates – subscription payable)

http://www.ukbmd.org.uk/index.php (Links to lots of birth, marriage and death resources)

http://www.british-genealogy.com/forums/archive/index.php/f-167.html (Lists of unwanted birth, marriage and death certificates that may assist your genealogical research)

http://www.interment.net/uk/index.htm (Births, marriages, deaths and wills including Boyd's Marriage Index; some services are by subscription)

http://www.british-genealogy.com/forums/forumdisplay.php?f=222 (General births, marriage and deaths information, including how to obtain certificates)

http://www.familyhistoryonline.net/ (Lots of searchable resources for family historians – registration required)

http://www.ancestry.co.uk (Search GRO registers for birth, marriages and deaths – pay to view) http://www.ancestry.co.uk/search/rectype/vital/epr/main.aspx (Search facility for parish and probate records)

http://www.findmypast.com (Search GRO registers – pay to view)

http://www.familyrelatives.org/ (A site that claims to hold over four million records – viewable by subscription)

http://www.BMDindex.co.uk/ (Search for BM&D certificates 1837-2005 – fee payable)

http://www.cornwall-opc-database.org/searchdb.php?dbname=burials (Search for Cornish birth, death or marriage certificates)

http://www.genuki.org.uk/big/eng/YKS/Misc/Transcriptions/NRY/MaltonMessenger1856BDM.html (Yorkshire BMD from the *Malton Messenger* newspaper 1856)

http://www.proni.gov.uk/ (Site for the Public Record Office of Northern Ireland)

PARISH & REGIONAL RECORDS

http://www.genuki.org.uk/search/ (Type 'parish registers' into the search engine to obtain over twelve thousand links to UK records)

http://prtsoc.org.uk/ (Web page of the Paris Register Transcription Society)

http://www.freereg.org.uk/search/index.htm (Search parish registers free)

http://www.parishregisters.co.uk (Selection of parish register transcripts)

http://www.parishregisteruklook-upexchange.co.uk/ (Parish register look-ups)

http://www.wirksworth.org.uk/ (Parish records site for Wirksworth, Derbyshire)

http://www.wirksworth.org.uk/REGS-02.htm (Derbyshire parish registers guide)

http://edenlinks.rootsweb.com/1gp/gerhard/INDEX.HTML (Cumberland parish record transcripts)

http://www.whitbyarchives.org.uk/ (Whitby Archives Heritage Centre, Yorkshire – genealogy records, resources and photographs for North Yorkshire and further afield))

http://www.england-in-particular.info/parishmaps/m-boundary.html (All about parish boundaries)

http://www.great-harwood.org.uk/genealogy/indexlinks/documents.htm (Wide range of genealogy documents for Great Harwood)

http://www.yesterdaysnames.co.uk/parishes.htm (Index of names found in old parish magazines – commercial site)

http://webs.lanset.com/azazella/cornish_database.html (Cornish records, transcripts and databases)

http://www.cornwall-opc-database.org/searchdb.php?dbname=baptisms (Search for Cornish baptisms)

http://ca.geocities.com/patriciablackburn2004/HeartsOfOak/returns6.html (Complete transcript of the Whitby 'non-parochial' registers at The National Archives)

http://www.norfolkfhs.org.uk/parishes/norfolkcontigparishes.htm (Contiguous parishes, what they are and how to use related information, plus parish search and links)

http://www.moonrakers.org.uk/files.asp (Download Wiltshire parish records)

http://freespace.virgin.net/tt.indexes/Bapt01y+.pdf (PDF format online baptism records for Wiltshire) http://www.parkhouse.org.uk/transcr/tcontent.htm (Devon and Somerset parish register transcriptions)

http://www.genuki.org.uk/big/eng/SOM/Wellington/Transcripts/index.html#baptisms (Baptism records for Wellington St John, Somerset 1683-1812)

BASTARDY EXAMINATIONS

http://freepages.genealogy.rootsweb.com/~mrawson/brasted2.html (Some early bastardy records from Brasted, Kent giving mother's name)

http://freepages.genealogy.rootsweb.com/~mrawson/brasted4.html (As above but indexed by father's name)

MARRIAGES

http://genuki.cs.ncl.ac.uk/StCathsTranscriptions/ (A selection of transcriptions from St Catherine's marriage Index up to 1861)

http://www.sog.org.uk/vg/vgnames.htm (Search the Vicar General's marriage licence index 1694-1850)

http://www.old-liverpool.co.uk/marriages.html (Liverpool marriages)

http://www.genuki.org.uk/big/eng/SOM/Wellington/Transcripts/index.html#marriages (Marriage records from Wellington St John, Somerset 1683-1783)

http://www.geocities.com/Athens/Aegean/7023/clandestine.html (Tutorial relating to clandestine marriages)

http://www.geocities.com/Athens/Aegean/7023/clandestine.html (All about clandestine marriages)

http://www.cornwall-opc-database.org/searchdb.php?dbname=marriages (Search for Cornish marriages)

http://www.dur.ac.uk/j.m.hutson/tudhoe/md1696.html (Marriage Duty tax returns – Tudhoe, Durham 1696)

http://www.originsnetwork.com/help/helpbo-bmi.htm (Boyd's Marriage Index - explanation and how to use it)

http://genealogy-search-swicki.eurekster.com/boyd's+marriage+index/ (Links to various Boyd's Marriage Index pages)

http://website.lineone.net/~jjoiner/mindex/mindex.html (Marriages database for Northern England)

http://www.genuki.org.uk/mwi/ (Ted Wildy's marriage witness index)

http://www.genuki.org.uk/big/eng/YKS/Misc/Transcriptions/YKS/PaversIndex.html (Paver's Marriage Licence extracts for Yorkshire 1567-1628)

http://www.lawsons.ca/marriages/_mar_index.html (Isle of Man marriages)

MARRIAGE LICENCE ALLEGATIONS

http://www.originsnetwork.com/help/popup-aboutbo-mla2.htm (How to search the index, 1640-1850)

DIVORCE

http://www.familyhistory.uk.com/index.php?option=com_content&task=view&id=548&Itemid=29 UK guide to divorce records)

http://www.nationalarchives.gov.uk/catalogue/Leaflets/ri2289.htm (Guide and index references to divorces after 1858 from The National Archives)

http://www.nas.gov.uk/guides/divorce.asp (Scottish guide to divorce records)

http://www.whosdatedwho.com/celebrities/people/records/most-divorces.htm (Celebrity divorces)

BURIALS, CEMETERY, GRAVEYARD & CREMATORIUM RECORDS

http://www.memorialinscriptions.org.uk/ (UK National Archive of Memorial Inscriptions – free search but pay to view details)

http://www.findagrave.com/ (Search here for graves of the ordinary and the famous)

http://lists.rootsweb.com/index/intl/UK/UK-CEMETERIES.html (Mailing list and archives search for UK cemeteries)

http://www.british-genealogy.com/resources/graves/ (All about monumental inscriptions, also known as MIs)

http://www.cwgc.org/ (Search the Commonwealth War Graves Commission's records)

http://www.srgw.demon.co.uk/CremSoc/LegalEtc/Archives.html (Archives of the Cremation Society)

http://www.gravestonephotos.com/public/faq.php (Gravestone photograph project)

http://www.rootsweb.com/~engcemet/ (England Tombstone Project – countrywide links)

http://www.gravestonephotos.com/index.php (Gravestone photograph archives listed by county and by surname)

http://web.ukonline.co.uk/thursday.handleigh/genealogy/graves/grave-imagery.htm (Gravestone symbols and their meanings)

http://www.isle-of-wight-memorials.org.uk/ (Isle of Wight memorials and monuments)

http://www.cornwall-opc-database.org/searchdb.php?dbname=burials (Search for Cornish burials)

http://www.sfhg.org.uk/mipageA.html (Index to burial names found in Suffolk)

http://www.haverhill-uk.com/pages/burial-records-137.htm (Burials at Haverhill)

http://www.isle-of-man.com/manxnotebook/famhist/pregs/lnbu1718.htm (List of 18th century Isle of Man burials)

http://www.manchester.gov.uk/opservices/bereave/onlinefaqs.htm (Manchester burial records online – paid service)

http://freepages.genealogy.rootsweb.com/~mrawson/gwichbur.html (List of Greenwich burials, 1820-1821)

http://www.cefnpennar.com/church_list.htm (Welsh headstone and memorial inscription project)

http://www.cefnpennar.com/monuments.htm (Pictures of Welsh memorials)

http://www.gravetext.co.uk/Quaker_Burials/Quaker_Burials_at_Winnows_Hill.pdf (Northumberland Quaker burials and other records – PDF format)

http://www.genuki.org.uk/big/eng/SOM/Wellington/Transcripts/index.html#burials (Burial records – Wellington St John, Somerset 1683-1812)
http://www.proni.gov.uk/records/graves.htm (Irish guide to gravestone inscriptions)
http://www.historyfromheadstones.com/index.php?home (Irish gravestones and graveyards)
http://www.interment.net/data/gib/trafalgar/index.htm (List of burials in Gibraltar, 1798-1814)
http://members.ozemail.com.au/~clday/cem.htm (European cemeteries in India)
http://www.gravestonestudies.org/archives.htm (Archives of the US Association for Gravestone Studies)
http://geneasearch.com/cemeteries.htm (Trace ancestors buried in cemeteries in the USA)
http://www.interment.net/ (Graveyard transcriptions from around the world sorted by country)

BRASS MEMORIALS

http://www.medievalgenealogy.org.uk/sources/brasses1.shtml (Links to monumental brasses on the internet)
http://www.mbs-brasses.co.uk/ (Site dedicated to monumental brass memorials and engraved plates)

CORONERS COURTS (INQUESTS)

http://www.nationalarchives.gov.uk/search/quick_search.aspx?search_text=coroners (Using coroners' records at The National Archives)
http://www.kcl.ac.uk/depsta/law/research/coroners/contents.html (Kings College coroners' law resources)
http://mysite.wanadoo-members.co.uk/longtown19/deathsinquest.html (Sudden deaths and inquests in the Carlisle area, 1800-1847)
http://www.salford.gov.uk/living/bmd/historysearch/genealogy/coronerrecords.htm (Where to find Lancashire inquest records)
http://www.edenlinks.co.uk/RECORDS/FAR/FAREX.HTM (Selection of online Kendal and district inquests, 1080-1700)

OBITUARIES

http://archiver.rootsweb.com/th/index/ENGLISH-OBITS (Search Rootsweb's UK obituary-sharing message archives)
http://politics.guardian.co.uk/politicsobituaries/0,1441,562536,00.html (*Guardian* newspaper site for political obituaries)
http://catless.ncl.ac.uk/Obituary/ (Obituaries with links to other 'death' subjects)
http://www.old-liverpool.co.uk/marriages.html (Liverpool obituaries)
http://www.ancestry.co.uk/search/obit/?us&dbid=7545 (Search for US obituaries)

CENSUS RETURNS

National census records that are so useful to family historians began in 1841 and have continued to be taken on a ten yearly basis since that time, excluding 1941 during World War II. These are invaluable for tying down families to particular locations and in giving us such vital details as names, ages, occupations and places of birth. Censuses taken before 1841 have often not survived, and normally did not contain information useful for genealogical purposes – some transcriptions have been placed on the net. The release of census material has been governed by the 100-year-rule, which means that at the time of writing the 1901 census is the latest that has been made available for research, although the 1911 census will be released early following public demand.

PRE-1841 CENSUSES

http://edenlinks.rootsweb.com/1gp/RECORDS/CC/CCINDEX.HTM (Constable's census 1787, Westmorland only)
http://www.origins.org.uk/genuki/NFK/places/y/yarmouth/census1803.shtml (Names in the Great Yarmouth population census, 1803)
http://www.staffs.ac.uk/schools/humanities_and_soc_sciences/census/vichome.htm (1831 census, free data)
http://www.origins.org.uk/genuki/NFK/norfolk/census/pre1841.shtml (Pre-1841 Norfolk censuses)

UNDERSTANDING THE NATIONAL CENSUS

http://www.familyrecords.gov.uk/topics/census_2.htm#1841 (Useful list of what information will be found on the census for any given year)
http://www.staffs.ac.uk/schools/humanities_and_soc_sciences/census/cebs.htm (Site that explains how censuses were completed, with tips on understanding the information that was gathered)
http://www.nationalarchives.gov.uk/pathways/census/main.htm (Interesting illustrated online historical study entitled '1901: Living at the time of the census')
http://genuki.cs.ncl.ac.uk/Transcriptions/DUR/CensusAbbrev.html (The most common abbreviations found in the census)
http://www.genealogy-links.co.uk/html/census.html (Exact dates of each census from 1801 to 1911 with search facility)
http://www.nationalarchives.ie/genealogy/censusrtns.html (Illustrations and explanations about various census forms)

ENGLAND & WALES FROM 1841

http://www.genuki.org.uk/big/Census.html (Genuki's own set of links to various census-related sites)
http://www.freecen.org.uk/ (Free census records online)
http://www.nationalarchives.gov.uk/census/ (National Archives' free search, pay to view)

http://www.1901censusonline.com/search.asp?wci=all_search&searchtype=16 (All online censuses)

http://www.ancestry.co.uk (Pay to view 1841 to 1901 census)

http://findmypast.com (Pay to view 1841 to 1891 census)

http://familyrelatives.com (Pay to view 1841 to 1891 census)

http://www.genuki.org.uk/big/census_place.html (Search and locate places mentioned in censuses)

http://www.gensource.com/census/c19l474.htm (Selective online census lists)

http://www.staffs.ac.uk/schools/humanities_and_soc_sciences/census/vichome.htm (1861 census free data)

http://1901census.rootschat.com/ (Private contributions from 1901 census with links)

SPECIFIC LOCATIONS

http://www.census-online.com/links/England/Durham/ (Durham and other area census details by county)

http://www.andrewspages.dial.pipex.com/matlock/cen-incl.htm (Matlock census records online)

http://www.genuki.org.uk/big/wal/CAE/Llandegai/Llandegai51.html (Complete transcription Llandegái, Wales, 1851)

http://www.genuki.org.uk/big/eng/GLS/Quenington/Census51.html (1851 census listing for Quenington, Gloucestershire)

http://www.angelfire.com/de/BobSanders/LpoolSailorsHome81.html (Census details of Liverpool Sailors' Home, 1881)

http://homepage.ntlworld.com/bandl.danby/1881CensusIndex.html (Census details for Skelton in Cleveland, 1881)

http://www.originsnetwork.com/help/helpio-census1841.aspx (Irish strays, 1841 census)

http://freepages.genealogy.rootsweb.com/~mrawson/chart1891.html (Census list from 1891 for Little Chart, Kent)

1851 ECCLESIASTICAL CENSUS

http://www.nationalarchives.gov.uk/catalogue/RdLeaflet.asp?sLeafletID=126&j=1 (Guide to the 1851 ecclesiastical census)

1881 CENSUS

http://www.familysearch.org (Free access to transcribed 1881 census)

http://www.1881-census.co.uk/ (1881 census on line – England and Wales by county)

http://www.censusuk.co.uk/ (1881 census search with links to other information; requires your email address)

http://www.lostcousins.com/ (Links researchers looking for the same relative using the UK and Canadian censuses of 1881) http://www.apex.net.au/~tmj/c81-adrs.htm (Aids to finding an address in the 1881 census)

IRISH CENSUS

http://www.censusfinder.com/ireland.htm (Irish census records)
http://www.rootsweb.com/~fianna/guide/census.html (All about Irish census records and substitutes)

SCOTTISH CENSUS

http://scotlandspeople.gov.uk (Official site, links to Scottish census 1841-1901)
http://www.censusfinder.com/scotland.htm (Scottish census resources)
http://www.genealogyinc.com/search/census_scotland_1841.html (Search Scottish censuses - commercial site)
http://www.ancestry.co.uk (Scottish census returns, pay to view)

SHIPPING

http://1881.ships.breccen.com/1881/1881_ship.html (Free Welsh shipping census search 1881)
http://homepage.ntlworld.com/jeffery.knaggs/RNShips.html (Index of Royal Navy ships and their positions, captains etc at the 1901 census)

CHARITIES, INSTITUTIONS & THE POOR

Most towns, and even villages, had their own charitable institutions, such as almshouses and orphanages, and of course, workhouses. The latter were part of the Poor Law system, which also created records of, for instance, settlement and removal. The records that survive have usually been deposited at local archives, record offices and libraries. Because they will often be listed under their local names on the internet, it may be necessary to search for them individually.

ALL INSTITUTIONS

http://www.institutions.org.uk/index.html (The comprehensive Rossbret Institutions site)
http://rylibweb.man.ac.uk/data1/dg/methodist/poor/list.html (View documents related to Methodism and the poor online)
http://www.old-liverpool.co.uk/snippets.html (Page with links to Liverpool institutions)

SURVEYS

http://booth.lse.ac.uk/ (Charles Booth's survey into life and labour in London 1886-1903)

ALMSHOUSES / CHARTERHOUSES

http://www.institutions.org.uk/almshouses/ (Website pages devoted to almshouses throughout the country)

http://homepage.ntlworld.com/jeffery.knaggs/I0248a.html (List of residents of the Charterhouse (Sutton's Hospital), East Finsbury, London in 1901)

BOARDS OF GUARDIANS (POOR LAW)

http://www.wirksworth.org.uk/BOARD.htm (Derbyshire Board of Guardians members)

http://www.genuki.org.uk/big/eng/YKS/Misc/Transcriptions/NRY/PickeringGuardiansIndex.html (Index to minutes of Board of Guardians and others – Pickering, Yorkshire 1800s)

http://www.genuki.org.uk/big/eng/LIN/Caistor/caistor_union_list.txt (Caistor Poor Law Guardians and actual records 1836-1846)

FOUNDLINGS

http://www.cichw.net/pmfound.html (Foundling Hospital website)

http://www.bbc.co.uk/radio4/womanshour/27_05_02/tuesday/info3.shtml (Listen online to a broadcast about abandoned babies)

http://www.24hourmuseum.org.uk/exh_gfx_en/ART28219.html (Love tokens left for foundlings, adding a pleasant note to otherwise sad stories)

http://www.24hourmuseum.org.uk/museum/SE000370.html (Website of the Foundling Museum, London)

http://www.bbc.co.uk/history/british/victorians/foundling_01.shtml (BBC account of Coram's Foundling institution)

http://www.ibdna.com/articles/Foundlings.htm (Using DNA in foundling cases)

ORPHANS, WAIFS & STRAYS

http://www.institutions.org.uk/orphanages/ (British orphanages listed by county as well as national organisations)

http://www.victorianlondon.org/dickens/dickens-charities.htm (List of names and addresses of Victorian London charities)

http://www.hiddenlives.org.uk/index.html (Lots of resources for researching orphans and waifs and strays including photos, documents and case files)

http://homepage.ntlworld.com/jeffery.knaggs/Instuts.html (Institutions in 1901 census with some lists of residents)

http://www.isle-of-man.com/manxnotebook/famhist/genealgy/chomes.htm (Children's homes in the Isle of Man) http://www.met-cityorphans.org.uk/history/archive.php (Details of the Metropolitan and City Police Orphanage archives)

http://homepage.ntlworld.com/jeffery.knaggs/l0012a.html (Orphanage of Mercy, Randolph Gardens, Kilburn, Paddington, London in 1901)

http://homepage.ntlworld.com/jeffery.knaggs/l0012c.html (St Vincent's Home for Desolate Roman Catholic Male Children, Paddington 1901)

http://homepage.ntlworld.com/jeffery.knaggs/l0012d.html (Victoria Orphanage, Shirland Road, Paddington 1901)

http://homepage.ntlworld.com/jeffery.knaggs/l0033f.html (National Industrial Home for Crippled Boys, Wrights Lane, Kensington 1901)

http://homepage.ntlworld.com/jeffery.knaggs/l0096k.html (Sisters of Charity of St Vincent de Paul, Carlisle Place, Westminster 1901)

http://homepage.ntlworld.com/jeffery.knaggs/l0106c.html (All Saints Home, 74-83 Margaret Street, Marylebone 1901)

http://homepage.ntlworld.com/jeffery.knaggs/l2392a.html (Homes for Pauper Children Beaufort and Summerhill Roads, St George, Bristol 1901)

http://homepage.ntlworld.com/jeffery.knaggs/l2364b.html (Staff and boys at the Home for Boys of the Bristol Union, Bristol 1901)

http://homepage.ntlworld.com/jeffery.knaggs/l0109c.html (St Vincent De Paul's Convent and Orphanage -9 Lower Seymour Street, Portman Square, Marylebone 1901)

http://www.berksfhs.org.uk/journal/Dec2002/OrphansAtBearwood.htm (Orphans at Bearwood, the Merchant Seamen's Orphan Asylum, with pictures)

http://www.liverpool-genealogy.org.uk/Information/orphanages.htm (Names and details from Liverpool orphanage records)

REFUGES

http://homepage.ntlworld.com/jeffery.knaggs/l2387a.html (List of those at the Bath Road Refuge for Penitent Women, Bristol 1901)

SCHOOLS FOR THE DISABLED

http://www.institutions.org.uk/special_schools/index.htm ('Special Schools' sorted by location)

TRAMPS & VAGRANTS

http://www.wirksworth.org.uk/Board-2.htm#44 (Lists of Victorian tramps and vagrants in Derbyshire, plus other records)

WORKHOUSES & POOR LAW RELIEF

http://www.genuki.org.uk/search/ (Type in the words POOR LAW into this search engine to find almost 4,000 links to Poor Law resources throughout Britain and the UK) http://www.workhouses.org.uk/ (Website devoted to all aspects of the subject of workhouses and the poor)

http://www.institutions.org.uk/workhouses/ (Workhouse website – search for all Poor Law Union workhouses in Britain plus interesting links to other subjects relating to the poor at that time)

http://users.ox.ac.uk/~peter/workhouse/index.html (Information regarding everything to do with workhouses)

http://www.gmcro.co.uk/cs/poor_law_records.htm (All about Poor Law records with links to other resources)

http://www.nationalarchives.gov.uk/documentsonline/workhouse.asp (Search documents from Southwell Workhouse 1834-1871)

http://www.nas.gov.uk/guides/poor.asp (Records of the poor in the Scottish National Archives)

http://homepage.ntlworld.com/jeffery.knaggs/l1549a.html (Staff and residents at North Witchford Union Workhouse, Doddington, Cambridgeshire in 1901)

http://www.stevebulman.f9.co.uk/cumbria/carlisle_workhouse_f.html (List of Carlisle workhouses)

http://www.sussexrecordsociety.org.uk/plhome.asp?an=&ap= (Database of Poor Law records in West Sussex)

http://www.northamptonshire.gov.uk/Community/record/Poorlaw.htm (Guide to the surviving Northamptonshire Poor Law records)

http://www.workhouses.org.uk/index.html?map/swest.shtml (Map of Poor Law Unions in South West England with links to other areas)

http://www.genuki.org.uk/big/eng/LIN/Boston/boston_union_list.txt (Boston, Lincolnshire, Poor Law records from 1837 onwards)

http://www.genuki.org.uk/big/eng/LIN/Stamford/stamford_union_list.txt (Stamford Poor Law records 1835-1838)

http://www.genuki.org.uk/big/eng/YKS/Misc/Transcriptions/NRY/PickeringWorkhouseIndex.html (Residents of Pickering Workhouse, Yorkshire searchable by name 1800s and 1900s)

http://www.genuki.org.uk/big/eng/LIN/poorhouse.html (List of Lincolnshire poorhouses and almshouses)

SETTLEMENT & REMOVAL ORDERS

http://web.ukonline.co.uk/ennever/stories/richard.htm (Explanation of the Poor Law settlement and removal order system)

http://freepages.genealogy.rootsweb.com/~mrawson/brasted1.html (Some Kent settlement and removal order listings)

http://freepages.genealogy.rootsweb.com/~mrawson/removals.html (Index of over 500 appeals against removal orders in West Kent 1758-1788)

http://www.genuki.org.uk/big/eng/DBY/Barlow/Settlement.html (Transcriptions of settlement certificates in Barlow, Derbyshire 1671-1832)

CHARTERS, CARTULARIES & HISTORIC PUBLIC RECORDS

Charters, the legal documents that recorded the conditions of grants of land, property or other rights, are in effect the old equivalent of the modern deed. Cartularies on the other hand are documentary records (including charters and title deeds) kept by monasteries and sometimes by lay establishments. Many have now been deposited at record offices. Though they do not directly link to family trees, some include names, locations and other details that are invaluable to those tracing early ancestry. Records of this kind for specific individual abbeys or cities should be searched for using Google or other search engine, or the British History Online website below.

ALL CATEGORIES

http://www.british-history.ac.uk/ ('British History Online' with a vast collection of transcripts of ancient charters, cartularies and historic documentation)
http://hcl.harvard.edu/research/guides/medieval/microform/part4.html (Harvard College library - catalogues of charters, cartularies and other old documents and records)

CARTULARIES

http://paleo.anglo-norman.org/cart.html (Cartularies, their uses and faults)
http://www.medievalwriting.50megs.com/word/monasticcart.htm (Monastic cartularies)

CHARTERS

http://www.trin.cam.ac.uk/kemble/index.php?menuitem=6&pagename=06 (A site specialising in Anglo-Saxon charters)
http://medievalwriting.50megs.com/word/charter2.htm (Royal Charters)
http://www.medievalgenealogy.org.uk/sources/public.shtml#rec (Links to medieval public records available online)

PUBLIC RECORDS

http://www.medievalgenealogy.org.uk/sources/public.shtml#rec (Links to medieval public records available online)
http://en.wikipedia.org/wiki/Anglo-Saxon_Chronicle (All about the Anglo-Saxon Chronicle)

CHRONOLOGY

Knowing the chronology of events adds understanding to our family tree research, placing our ancestors firmly within an historical framework and, for instance, knowing the years when a king or queen reigned or how to read dates written in Roman numerals on an old document helps us date events exactly. There are a number of online aids.

AGE CALCULATOR

http://www.digitalhistory.co.uk/datecalc.aspx (Calculate someone's age at any census)

CALENDARS & DATES

http://www.british-genealogy.com/resources/info/sdates.html (Important dates in history for genealogists)

http://www.genfair.com/dates.htm (Researchers' guide to the Old and New Style calendars)

http://www.albion.edu/english/calendar/regnal.htm (Converts years of reigns of individual monarchs, eg 9 Geo. III, found in documents to actual years)

http://www.combs-families.org/combs/reference/regnal.htm (A list of regnal years)

http://www.ourtimelines.com/ (Generates a personal timeline chart for your family tree)

http://www.saintpatrickdc.org/ss/cal-ss.htm (Calendar of Saints' Days organised by date)

http://www.catholic.org/saints/stindex.php (Saints and Saints' Days listed)

http://www.albion.edu/english/calendar/style.htm (Convert Old Style calendar dates to New and vice versa)

http://www.chsbs.cmich.edu/Kristen_McDermott/ENG235/EM_calendar.htm (Early modern calendar with Saints' Days and festivals)

http://www.medievalgenealogy.org.uk/cal/medcal.shtml (A medieval calendar)

http://www.genuki.org.uk/big/easter/ (Lists the dates for Easter Sunday 1550-2049 and links to a calendar for each of those years)

http://medievalist.net/calendar/months.htm (Discover Saints' and religious days that were important to previous generations)

EVENTS

http://www.thebookofdays.com/calender.htm (Click any date to find the historical links and events connected to that date throughout history)

http://www.angelfire.com/de/BobSanders/TIME1.html (Historical events AD 122 to 1500)

http://www.angelfire.com/de/BobSanders/TIME2.html (ditto 1501-1900)

http://www.angelfire.com/de/BobSanders/TIME3.html (ditto 1900-1995)

ROMAN NUMERALS

http://www.guernsey.net/~sgibbs/roman.html (Easily convert numbers, dates etc, with links to old calendars)

CLANS

A clan is defined as a group of people united by kinship or descent from a common ancestor. Clans exist in many countries and more can be learned about them from the various websites listed below.

ALL CLANS WORLDWIDE

http://en.wikipedia.org/wiki/Clan (Explanation of clan systems together with links throughout the world by country)
http://www.clansearch.co.uk/Search.htm (Search for information about specific clans here)

IRISH CLANS

http://www.censusfinder.com/irish_surnames.htm (Irish clan and surname resources)
http://www.finditireland.com/links/irishclansites.html (Links to individual clan websites)

SCOTTISH CLANS

http://www.electricscotland.com/familytree/newsletters/index.htm (Links to clans and clan societies by name)
http://www.borderart.com/ (Clan maps and artwork – commercial site)
http://www.ancestralscotland.com/roots/beginning.html (Search for Scottish clans and surnames)
http://www.clansearch.co.uk/Clan%20Index.htm (Another clan search page)
http://www.gengateway.com/index.cfm?GID=22 (Links to various documents including clans of Scotland)

JAPANESE CLANS

http://www.samurai-archives.com/clanindex.html (Family trees of Japanese clan names)

COATS OF ARMS, HERALDRY, EMBLEMS & FLAGS

It should be remembered that coats of arms, contrary to popular opinion, were not issued to a family name, but instead to an individual person and his descendants. Consequently a number of people with the same surname will have different coats of arms and not everyone with that surname will be entitled to use those arms. Also listed below are some sites with resources for identifying flags, tartans and similar visual emblems.

ALL SUBJECTS

http://www.bubl.ac.uk/link/linkbrowse.cfm?menuid=11374 (A website with a vast range of family history links including supplementary material such as flags, tartans, history of names and similar subjects of interest to genealogists)

FLAGS

http://flagspot.net/flags/ (World flags reference site)

HERALDRY / COATS OF ARMS

http://www.college-of-arms.gov.uk/Faq.htm (All the answers you will need to questions about coats of arms and what arms have been granted to various families)
http://www.fotw.net/flags/vxt-hrld.html (Pictorial heraldic dictionary with links)
http://www.ihgs.ac.uk/ (Website of the Institute of Heraldic and Genealogical Studies)
http://www.heraldica.org/topics/glossary/ (Miscellaneous heraldic study links with glossary and dictionaries)
http://www.cyndislist.com/heraldry.htm#General (Lots of heraldry resources)
http://www.theheraldrysociety.com/ (Website of the Heraldry Society)
http://www.heraldry-scotland.co.uk/ (Scottish Heraldry Society site)
http://www.leitrim-roscommon.com/heraldry/heraldry.html (Gaelic Irish heraldry site)
http://www.heraldry.ca/ (Royal Heraldry Society of Canada)
http://www.digiserve.com/heraldry/ (Commercial site with links to free heraldry resources on the internet)
http://www.traceit.com/ (Commercial site with information on family names and related heraldic crests)

COPYRIGHT

Copying or using pictures and documentation of others when compiling family trees and on personal genealogical websites is subject to the laws of copyright. Often simply asking the owner for written permission will solve any problems. Sometimes the owner is not known or the original is very old and then further advice is needed.

http://ahds.ac.uk/copyrightfaq.htm (Frequently asked questions about British copyright are answered on this site)
http://www.ict4lt.org/en/en_copyright.htm (General guidelines on copyright)

DIRECTORIES

Directories provide valuable information, especially trade directories which give business names and addresses and quite often home addresses also. Because they were published on a regular basis, they can help family historians not only locate their ancestor's business but also determine the years the business was in operation. Changes of location or name are also useful as an aid to estimating the date of death or retirement of proprietors. Most public libraries now have collections of these old local directories. Others can often be located on the net.

http://www.historicaldirectories.org/ (Trades directories for the UK, search by location, decade or keyword)
http://www.genuki.org.uk/search/ (Type the word 'directory' into the search engine to find thousands of trade and other directory resources for the UK and Ireland)
http://web.ukonline.co.uk/sheila.jones/trades.htm (Trade directories plus other resources)
http://www.staffs.ac.uk/schools/humanities_and_soc_sciences/census/vichome. htm (A selection of various regional directories)

DNA/GENETIC GENEALOGY

If you want to be at the cutting edge of ancestor research, then DNA and genetics can be used to trace not only your ancestors but also your family's historic geographical origins.

http://www.savin.org/dna/introduction.html (Introduction to genetic genealogy)
http://www.dnaancestryproject.com/ (Using DNA and genetics to trace your family tree)
http://www.oxfordancestors.com/ (Oxford Ancestors are the world's leading provider of DNA-based services for use in personal ancestry research)
http://www.ramsdale.org/adam.htm (Genetics and genealogy - technical articles)
http://www.scotsfamily.com/genetic-genealogy.htm (Genetic genealogy for Scotland with other links)
http://www.cambridgedna.com/genealogy-dna-genetic-genealogy.php (Cambridge DNA services for discovering genetic heritage)
http://www.ibdna.com/articles/Foundlings.htm (Using DNA in foundling and abandoned child cases)

DOMESDAY BOOK

The invasion of Britain in 1066 by William the Conqueror changed the face of Britain for ever. The changes in land ownership and the census of the land in 1086 gave us the 'Domesday Book', a collection of over 13,000 individual records listing land owners, previous land owners and their social status as well as their possessions at that time.

http://www.domesdaybook.co.uk/ (Online Domesday Book with search facility)
http://www.domesdaybook.net/ (Domesday Book research facilities)

http://www.fordham.edu/halsall/source/domesday1.html (All about the Domesday survey)

EDUCATION

Educational records can be difficult to locate on the internet, though school addresses, pictures, lists of staff and sometimes pupils can occasionally be found. A good tip is to try typing the name of the particular school in question or the education authority you are seeking into a search engine. Often this will bring up obscure websites or educational resources which do not appear on the major genealogy sites.

http://www.genuki.org.uk/search/ (Type 'school' or 'schools' into this search engine to access thousands of educational documents and resources)
http://www.proni.gov.uk/school/Educbord.htm (Department of Education of Northern Ireland research website)
http://www.nas.gov.uk/guides/education.asp (Guide to Scottish education records)
http://homepage.ntlworld.com/jeffery.knaggs/I0142c.html (Residents of Home and Colonial Training College, Grays Inn Lane, St Pancras, London 1901)
http://homepage.ntlworld.com/jeffery.knaggs/I1167b.html (Staff in residence at Royal Holloway College, Egham, Surrey in 1901 census)
http://homepage.ntlworld.com/jeffery.knaggs/I1170c.html (Staff and boys at Beaumont College, Priest Hill, Egham, Surrey in 1901 census)
http://homepage.ntlworld.com/jeffery.knaggs/I2370b.html (Staff and boys at the Clifton Certified Industrial School for Boys, Church Path, Clifton Wood, Bristol in 1901 census)
http://www.history.ac.uk/gh/christ1.htm (Guide to Guildhall records of the 'Bluecoat Schools')
http://www.liverpoolmuseums.org.uk/online/exhibitions/childhood/medals.asp (Guide explaining the Education Acts of 1876 and 1880; also the use of school attendance medals)
http://www.hertfordshire-genealogy.co.uk/data/education/schoolsandecucation.htm (Old photographs of Hertfordshire schools)
http://www.genuki.org.uk/big/eng/DBY/Newbold/SchoolMasters.html (List of Newbold, Derbyshire school teachers 1818-1887)
http://www.genuki.org.uk/big/eng/CAM/Ely/Schools.html (Schools in Ely, Cambridgeshire)
http://www.genuki.org.uk/big/eng/LIN/schoolteachers.html (List of 19th century Lincolnshire school teachers and headmasters)
http://www.genuki.org.uk/big/eng/YKS/Misc/Transcriptions/NRY/CroptonSchoolRegister.htm (Schoolmasters, Cropton, Yorkshire 1800s and early 1900s)
http://met.open.ac.uk/genuki/big/eng/BKM/Aylesbury/schools/grammar.html (Names associated with Aylesbury Grammar School 1678-1903)
http://www.kirkbymalham.info/KMI/kirkbymalham/kmfgschool.html (Website of

Kirkby Malham Grammar School with list of schoolmasters 1736-1873)
http://www.hertfordshire-genealogy.co.uk/data/education/stalbans-schools.htm (St Albans 19th century school staff)

ELECTION RECORDS

For those who had ancestors involved in the political processes, there are a number of sources available on the internet. Many are small documents listing voters or those eligible to vote in particular areas. As they are too numerous to list individually, they should be searched for specifically using a search engine such as Google. Poll books (1690s-1872) show how individuals voted and where they lived – if they had property in different parts of the county, certain people may be found listed more than once. Some poll books also contain speeches and statements written by candidates for election. Electoral registers date from 1832 to the present day, listing all those eligible to vote.

POLL BOOKS

http://www.genuki.org.uk/search/ (Enter the words 'poll books' for links to over 170 resources with poll book references throughout the UK and Ireland)
http://www.british-genealogy.com/resources/info/pollbooks.html (Illustrated guide to using poll books as genealogical aids)
http://www.westsussex.gov.uk/ccm/content/libraries-and-archives/record-office/family-history/poll-booksand-electoral-registers.en (Poll book records in West Sussex)
http://www.iwight.com/library/record_office/Types_of_Records/electora.asp (Isle of Wight poll book references)

ELECTIONS, ELECTORAL ROLLS & REGISTERS

http://www.genuki.org.uk/search/ (Search here for lists of electors from your own area using the words 'electors' or 'electoral roll' in the search box)
http://www.bl.uk/collections/social/spis_er.html (Advice on how to find and use old registers)
http://www.192.com (One of several commercial sites offering searches of 2002-2007 electoral registers)
http://www.british-history.ac.uk/search.asp?query1=elections (List of historic records concerning British elections from early times)
http://www.alba.org.uk/westminster/index.html (Historic lists of election records, government ministers etc)
http://www.iwight.com/library/record_office/Types_of_Records/electora.asp (List of Isle of Wight registers, some of which are indexed)
http://www.origins.org.uk/genuki/NFK/norfolk/voting/ (Links to documents concerning Norfolk voting registers)
http://www.celticcousins.net/ireland/galway1727.htm (Galway election list 1727)

EMIGRATION & IMMIGRATION

When individuals and sometimes whole families settled in other countries it can cause problems in tracing them. The documentation involved in their movements can, however, often lead a family historian on the road to finding them in a new location quite quickly. A number of family history sites and societies have transcribed some of these documents making the task of finding them much easier – see also under **SHIPPING**.

EMIGRANTS /IMMIGRANTS

http://www.genuki.org.uk/search/ (Type the words 'emigrant' or 'immigrant' into the search engine to find hundreds of resources – try also 'emigrants' or 'immigrants' for a different set of records)

http://nationalarchives.gov.uk/search (type 'emigration' or 'immigration' into the search engine for many links and resources)

http://www.familyrecords.gov.uk/topics (Official site with links for emigration and immigration)

http://www.castlegarden.org/ (Offers free access to an extraordinary database of information on 10 million immigrants to the USA 1830 to 1892)

http://www.ellisisland.org/search/index.asp (Search thousands of names of immigrants that arrived at Ellis Island, New York, USA)

http://www.theshipslist.com/pictures/welsh1.htm (Details about Welsh emigrants to Patagonia)

http://members.aol.com/rprost/passenger.html (Lists of emigrants to Australia, Canada, New Zealand, South Africa and USA by ship)

http://homepages.ihug.co.nz/~tonyf/ (Website dedicated to pioneers and early settlers in New Zealand)

http://sa-passenger-list.za.net/index.php (South Africa resources)

http://homepage.ntlworld.com/inth/ (British settlers in Argentina, with name search)

http://www.eminorame.karoo.net/ (Emigrants from Yorkshire and Durham in the 1700s)

http://www.ubishops.ca/geoh/settlem/phases.htm (British settlement in the Eastern Townships 1820-1850 plus American and French settlers)

http://www.abdn.ac.uk/emigration/user-guide.html (Database of Scottish emigrants)

http://www.scotsgenealogy.com/online/early_scots_at_montreal.htm (Early Scots in Montreal)

http://www.genealogy-quest.com/collections/walloons.html (Walloons and French who emigrated to Virginia 1621)

http://www.movinghere.org.uk/galleries/histories/default.htm# (Resources for Caribbean, Jewish, Irish and South Asian immigrants)

http://www.everygeneration.co.uk/ (Genealogy links for black family history in Britain)

CHILD MIGRANTS

http://www.childmigrantstrust.com/ (Site dedicated to the compulsory migration of children from Britain to Australia, Canada and other parts of the Commonwealth)

http://www.ncvcco.org/our_work_projects_record.asp?title=Child+Migrant+Central
+Information+Index&id=22 (Child Migrant Central Information Index site)
http://www.dh.gov.uk/en/Publicationsandstatistics/Publications/
PublicationsPolicyAndGuidance/DH_4006199 (Dept of Health website with
downloadable information)
http://www.bbc.co.uk/radio4/history/child_migrants.shtml (Listen to BBC broadcasts
online regarding these child migrants)
http://www.nch.org.uk/information/index.php?i=195 (How to access National
Children's Charity records on compulsory child migrants)
http://www.naa.gov.au/fsheets/FS147.html (About child migrant records held in
Sydney, Australia)
http://www.aph.gov.au/library/intguide/sp/childmigrantuk.htm (Australian Government
site with links)
http://ist.uwaterloo.ca/~marj/genealogy/homeadd.html (Young immigrants to Canada
with links)
http://freepages.genealogy.rootsweb.com/~britishhomechildren/ (Site dedicated to
Canada's '100,000 invisible child immigrants' a.k.a. the British Home Children)
http://www.collectionscanada.ca/02/02011003_e.html (Search the Canadian Archives
for British Home Children)
http://www.automatedgenealogy.com/uidlinks/BhcList.jsp (Alphabetical listing linked
to the 1901 census regarding the British Home Children)

NATURALIZATION RECORDS

http://nationalarchives.gov.uk/search (Type 'naturalization' into the search engine for
information and record sources)
http://www.movinghere.org.uk/galleries/roots/asian/migration/naturalization.htm
(What records are available and how to access them)
http://www.ancestry.co.uk/search/db.aspx?dbid=3826 (Search Minnesota, USA,
naturalization records 1854-1957; commercial site)
http://home.att.net/~wee-monster/naturalizationrecords.html (Family history guide to
US naturalization)

FAMILY HISTORY SOCIETIES & FAIRS

Family History Societies, known in genealogical circles as FHSs, form perhaps the largest
and fastest growing interconnected social membership group in Britain, and indeed the
world. Members collect and exchange information as well as compiling books, lists
and pamphlets regarding their own areas of interest. Lots of these are available for sale
whilst others are put on the web for free consultation. Most FHSs are members of the
Federation of Family History Societies (FFHS); though this is not always the case, so it
is always worth checking with your local library or telephone directory to see if smaller
local groups are meeting in your own area or in the region that you are researching.

http://www.ffhs.org.uk/members2/contacting.php (FFHS website – find a Family History Society in your area or in Australia, Canada, New Zealand & USA)
http://www.genuki.org.uk/Societies/ (Genuki's links to foreign and specialist FHSs)
http://www.ffhs.org.uk/General/Members/Other.htm#6ROL (Overseas and specialist FHS contacts)
http://www.genuki.org.uk/Societies/England.html (Genuki's list of English Family History Societies listed by county)
http://www.genuki.org.uk/Societies/Wales.html (Genuki's list of Welsh Family History Societies)
http://www.genuki.org.uk/Societies/Scotland.html (Genuki's list of Scottish Family History Societies)
http://www.genuki.org.uk/Societies/IsleOfMan.html (Genuki's list of IOM Family History Societies)
http://www.genuki.org.uk/Societies/Ireland.html (Genuki's list of Irish Family History Societies
http://www.genuki.org.uk/Societies/ChannelIslands.html (Genuki's list of Channel Islands Family History Societies)
http://one-name.org (Guild of One-Name Studies website)
http://www.ffhs.org.uk/members2/onename.php (Find a One-Name Society researching your own family surname)

FAMILY HISTORY FAIRS

http://members.aol.com/aquarterma/familyhistoryfairs.html (Find out how to visit a family history fair and when and where they will be held)
http://geneva.weald.org.uk/ (List of forthcoming family history events in the UK)

FIRE INSURANCE

Insurance documents and certificates provide names, addresses and details of the property insured, all of which can give family historians an insight into their ancestor's background and lifestyles whether on a business or personal footing.

http://www.history.ac.uk/gh/fire.htm (How to use Fire Insurance records at the Guildhall Library)
http://www.history.ac.uk/gh/sun.htm (How to access the online Sun Fire Office policy registers 1811-1835)

FREEMEN, GUILDS & LIVERY COMPANIES

Traditionally, Freemen had the right to elect the mayor, sheriff and aldermen of their town or city and to stand as Parliamentary representative. Until the 1800s normally one could only become a Freeman by one of three processes, namely through birth, through apprenticeship to another Freeman or by appointment. The position had other privileges, depending on which town, city or borough was concerned, mostly with regards to business or carrying out a trade. Guilds were associations of craftsmen and their records go back to medieval times – in London they were known as Livery Companies.

http://www.domesdaybook.net/helpfiles/hs2900.htm (History of the title of Freemen)
http://www.middle-ages.org.uk/medieval-london-guilds.htm (All about medieval Guilds)
http://simmonsgallery.co.uk/2001site/medals/Livery/liverymedals_6.htm (Illustrations of Guild medals, marks etc)
http://www.cheshire.gov.uk/Recordoffice/Freemen/ Search here for information about Freemen in Chester)
http://www.exeter.gov.uk/index.aspx?articleid=3470 (Information about Freemen in Essex)
http://www.muthergrumble.co.uk/issue05/mg0506.htm (Durham Freemen)
http://www.communigate.co.uk/york/freemenofyork/ (Freemen and Guilds of York)
http://www.lancaster.gov.uk/General.asp?id=SX9452-A78083B7&cat=832 (Roll of Freemen of City of Lancaster 1887-1982)
http://freepages.genealogy.rootsweb.com/~mrawson/free.html (Maidstone Freemen list 1694-1842)
http://www.guild-freemen-london.co.uk/help.php (Guild of Freemen of London)
http://www.cityoflondon.gov.uk/Corporation/leisure_heritage/livery/linklist.htm (Alphabetical list of London Livery Companies, with links)

GENEALOGICAL RESEARCH SERVICES

Many family history websites list or recommend professional family history researchers who will carry out genealogical research on your behalf. Regional libraries, archives and heritage centres are also useful in locating professional researchers, whose fees vary widely depending on their qualifications or geographical research areas.

http://www.agra.org.uk/ (Association of Genealogists and Researchers in Archives)
http://genealogypro.com/ (Find professional genealogists and specialised researchers here)
http://www.nationalarchives.gov.uk/irlist/ (The National Archives advice on finding a researcher)

GENEALOGY CHAT ROOMS, FORUMS, LOOK UPS, MESSAGE BOARDS & MAILING LISTS

These facilities allow family history researchers to make contact, chat, leave general enquiries, submit answers or place other material for anyone else to read. Chat Rooms allow individuals to talk on line about a specific subject, in this case genealogy. Many are linked to well known genealogy sites and they are quite useful for exchanging information and experiences for those who like this type of communication. It should always be remembered that though there are generally few problems with using these sites, it is often difficult to verify who you are talking to on internet chat lines and users should be extremely careful about giving out their name and address or other personal details to contacts. Genealogical mailing lists are regular bulletins sent direct to your computer via e-mail. Most are free and are useful ways of keeping up with family history news and research, whilst Look-up sites provide a means of other people looking up information for you in family history records that they have access to.

CHAT

http://www.looking4kin.com/ (A general family tree link site with chat facilities)

FORUMS

http://genforum.genealogy.com/ (Search for a forum that interests you)
http://www.uk-genealogy.org.uk/phpBB2/index.php (Lots of genealogy forums to choose from, all listed by regional interest)
http://genforum.genealogy.com/medieval/ (Medieval family history forum)

LOOK-UPS

http://www.genuki.org.uk/search/ (Type 'look-up' into the Genuki search engine to find over 5,000 regional, general and specialist look-up links)
http://www.parishregisteruklook-upexchange.co.uk/ (Parish register look-ups)
http://www.geocities.com/Heartland/Ranch/5973/london.htm (London look-ups)
http://members.aol.com/vsena/knox/LookUps.html (Look-ups for names etc)

MESSAGE BOARDS

http://boards.rootsweb.com/ (Helps you find a message board for any genealogical subject)
http://www.missing-you.net/Genealogy.php (Genealogy-based missing persons message board to find details, photos etc of lost or dead relatives)

MAILING LISTS

http://lists.rootsweb.com/ (Find a family history list that matches your own area of research – eg police, merchant navy, etc – and subscribe to it or alternatively search old lists for genealogical information)

http://www.genuki.org.uk/indexes/MailingLists.html (Another large selection of lists you can subscribe to)

http://freespace.virgin.net/genealogical.collections/cjmlists.htm (Explanation on using mailing lists with a selection of links to choose from)

http://www.rootsweb.com/~jfuller/gen_mail_country-unk-sct.html (Mailing lists dedicated to Scottish interests)

GENEALOGY MAGAZINES

Family history magazines are a good source of tips and information for tracing family trees. Some include databases of information in either printed form or on free CDs given away with each issue. These are some of the major genealogy magazine websites.

http://www.ancestorsmagazine.co.uk/ (*Ancestors* magazine – UK)
http://www.familyhistorymonthly.com (*Family History Monthly* – UK)
http://www.family-tree.co.uk/ (*Family Tree Magazine* and *Practical Family History* – UK)
http://www.yourfamilytreemag.co.uk/ (*Your Family Tree Magazine* –UK)
http://www.scotsgenealogy.com/magazine.htm (*Scottish Genealogist* - UK)
http://www.sog.org.uk/genmag/genmag.shtml (*Genealogists' Magazine* - journal of the Society of Genealogists – UK)
http://www.aftc.com.au/ (*Australian Family Tree Connections* – Australia)
http://www.familytreemagazine.com/ (*Family Tree Magazine* – USA)
http://www.genealogymagazine.com/ (*Genealogy Magazine* – USA)
http://www.familychronicle.com/ (*Family Chronicle* – USA)
http://internet-genealogy.com/author_notes.htm (*Internet Genealogy* - Canada)

HOSPITALS & ASYLUMS

Hospital records are notoriously hard to get hold of and access may be restricted for reasons of confidentiality. You may need to carry out a number of searches in order to find the whereabouts of specific records – below are samples of the types the diligent researcher could find. See also under **OCCUPATIONS** for medical, nursing and midwifery staff.

ALL RECORDS

http://www.nationalarchives.gov.uk/hospitalrecords/ (National Archives' database of hospital resources, including the old asylums)

http://www.medicalmuseums.org (London's hospital museums and archives, with links to websites)

HOSPITALS

http://www.institutions.org.uk/hospitals/index.html (Hospitals, sanatoriums etc listed by location)

http://genuki.org.uk/search (Type 'hospitals' in the search engine)

http://www.redcross.org.uk/standard.asp?id=2623&cachefixer (British Red Cross Museum and Archives with search facility to locate field hospitals etc)

http://homepage.ntlworld.com/jeffery.knaggs/l0109b.html (Patients and staff list of Casualty Ward, 86 East Street, Marylebone, London in 1901)

http://homepage.ntlworld.com/jeffery.knaggs/l0259a.html (Patients and staff of City of London Lying-In Hospital, City Road, Finsbury, London 1901)

http://homepage.ntlworld.com/jeffery.knaggs/l0612c.html (Patients and staff of Isolation Hospital, Mandora Barracks (Aldershot), Surrey 1901)

http://homepage.ntlworld.com/jeffery.knaggs/l0971c.html (Patients and staff of Infirmary for W' Sussex and E' Hampshire, Broyle Road Chichester in 1901)

http://homepage.ntlworld.com/jeffery.knaggs/l1306b.html (Patients and staff at Hertford General Hospital, North Road, Hertford in 1901)

ASYLUMS

http://www.institutions.org.uk/asylums/england/english_asylums.htm (Locate English asylums by county)

http://www.institutions.org.uk/asylums/wales/welsh_asylums.htm (List of Welsh asylums located by county)

http://www.institutions.org.uk/asylums/lunacy_commissioners.htm (Details and reports of the Lunacy Commissioners)

http://www.genuki.org.uk/search (Type 'asylums' into the search engine)

http://www.hertfordshire-genealogy.co.uk/data/topics/t070-long-stay-hospitals.htm (The 'long stay' hospitals of St Albans area)

http://www.hertfordshire-genealogy.co.uk/data/occupations/mad-houses.htm (Asylums in St Albans and Harpenden with names and links)

http://www.hertfordshire-genealogy.co.uk/data/answers/answers-2003/ans-0305-taylor.htm (19th century asylums near Watford)

http://yourarchives.nationalarchives.gov.uk/index.php?title=Broadmoor_Asylum (Tips on finding asylum records with links)

http://www.genuki.org.uk/big/eng/LIN/poorasylum.html (Page for researching Lincolnshire asylums)

http://genuki.cs.ncl.ac.uk/DEV/DevonIndexes/Asylum1880.html (Residents of Devon County Asylum 1880-1881)

http://www.fifefhs.org/Photos/almanacs/1913/asylum.htm (Picture of the Fife & Kinross Asylum football team with links to other sources)

http://www.mdx.ac.uk/WWW/STUDY/01.htm#7 (All you need to know about the Lunacy Commission with lots of links)
http://www.institutions.org.uk/asylums/scotland/edinburgh_asylums.htm (Brief details of Edinburgh asylum)

LAND & PROPERTY

Inheritance and land ownership have always been strictly governed by law in Britain; consequently records have been kept which stretch back to medieval times and beyond. Local *tithe* records are useful if your ancestor owned or resided on the land he worked; the Tithe Commutation Act of 1836 ensured the recording of the names of landowners and occupiers for most parishes throughout the country. *Field names* are also useful in pinpointing farmhouses and other buildings and in researching land sales and disputes. In the 12th century a procedure evolved for ending legal actions or disputes by an agreement known as *final concords* (or *fines*); by the 13th century the fine had become a popular way of conveying freehold property and the legal action involved was merely a device initiated by both parties to facilitate the transfer – the *feet of fines* were simply the portion of the document held by the court. See also **LAW & ORDER** and **MANORIAL RECORDS**.

ALL CATEGORIES

http://www.genuki.org.uk/search/ (Type the words 'land records' or 'land' separately, into this Genuki search engine to find over 5,000 local resources to choose from)

EXCHEQUER RECORDS

http://www.nationalarchives.gov.uk/search/quick_search.aspx (Search The National Archives resources)
http://www.history.ac.uk/cmh/exchequer.html (Medieval Exchequer records guide)
http://www.londonancestor.com/leighs/crt-excheq.htm (Informative website with some good links)
http://www.nas.gov.uk/guides/exchequer.asp (Guide to Scottish Exchequer Records)

FEET OF FINES

http://www.british-history.ac.uk/search.asp?query1=%22feet+of+fines%22 (Links to Feet of Fines in UK with transcriptions)
http://www.medievalgenealogy.org.uk/fines/index.shtml (Explanation of the Feet of Fines legal procedure with links)
http://freespace.virgin.net/doug.thompson/BraoseWeb/family/feet2.html (Historic example and transcription of a Feet of Fine)

http://www.medievalgenealogy.org.uk/fines/abstracts/CP_25_1_44_60.shtml
(Extracts from some Devon Feet of Fines)

REGISTRY OF DEEDS

http://www.landsearch.net/services.asp (Land Registry deeds search – commercial site)

http://www.proni.gov.uk/records/deeds.htm (Northern Ireland registry, useful to genealogists because many wills were destroyed in 1922)

http://www.archives.wyjs.org.uk/index.asp?pg=rod.html (West Yorkshire Registry of Deeds)

http://www.eastriding.gov.uk/libraries/archives/pdf/Register_of_Deeds.pdf (How to use the East Riding of Yorkshire Registry of Deeds)

http://www.gov.im/registries/general/deedsandpro.xml (Isle of Man Registry of Deeds site)

http://www.nas.gov.uk/guides/deeds.asp (Scottish Registry of Deeds)

RETURNS OF OWNERS OF LAND

http://www.genuki.org.uk/search/ (Type 'return of owners' into this Genuki search engine to access over 900 resources dealing with land ownership)

http://www.uk-genealogy.org.uk/datafiles/landtaxsearch.html (Search the returns of Owners of Land 1873 transcriptions – incomplete but growing database)

http://www.thornburypump.myby.co.uk/1873/ (Search Norfolk returns)

http://www.genuki.org.uk/big/wal/GreatLandowners.html (Welsh landowners)

http://www.cefnpennar.com/ang1873land/index.htm (List of landowners in Anglesey, 1873)

http://www.cefnpennar.com/ebay/irish_landowners.htm (Irish landowner returns 1873)

http://www.cefnpennar.com/ebay/scottish_landowners.htm (Scottish landowner returns 1873)

TITHES & ENCLOSURES

http://www.nationalarchives.gov.uk/catalogue/RdLeaflet.asp?sLeafletID=100&j=1 (National Archives guide to tithes and enclosures)

http://www.genuki.org.uk/search/ (Type the word 'tithe' into this search engine to access almost 2,000 resources)

http://www.british-history.ac.uk/search.asp?query1=tithe (Records and resources from British History On-Line)

http://www.devon.gov.uk/tithe_records (Tithe records in Devon)

http://www.kentarchaeology.org.uk/Research/Maps/Maps%20intro.htm (Kent maps and tithe award schedules)

http://www.tithemaps.org.uk/ (North Hampshire tithe map project)

http://www.devon.gov.uk/tithe_records (Devon tithes and map research facilities)

http://www.historic-maps.norfolk.gov.uk/emap/EMapExplorer.
asp?PID=6&MTY=2&BID=0 (Norfolk tithe information and maps)
http://www.dcda.org.uk/TitheApps/TITHEWCC.htm (Dorset tithe apportionments)
http://worcestershire.whub.org.uk/home/wcc-arch-tithe-maps.html (Worcestershire tithe and enclosure project)

FIELD NAMES

http://www.hartlandforum.co.uk/hartsoc/placenames.htm (Study and explanation of field names)
http://c.cater.users.btopenworld.com/HTMLFiles/english_field_names.html (Short essay on English field names with examples)
http://www.smr.herefordshire.gov.uk/hfn/db.php (Herefordshire field name database)
http://www.st-andrews.ac.uk/institutes/sassi/spns/field-names.htm (Scottish field names)
http://www.polkadotmittens.co.uk/names/field_names.html (Orkney field and place names)
http://www.bbc.co.uk/wales/mid/sites/lampeter/pages/jenmathias3.shtml (BBC site with discussion of Welsh field names)
http://www.burtonbradstock.org.uk/History/Old%20Maps/Field%20Names.htm (Example of a map showing field names)

VALUATION RECORDS

https://secure.nationalarchives.gov.uk/catalogue/leaflets/ri2153.htm (Guide to UK valuation records in The National Archives)
http://www.proni.gov.uk/records/valuatn.htm (How to access valuation records in Northern Ireland)
http://www.nas.gov.uk/guides/valuationRolls.asp (Guide to valuation records in Scotland)

LAW & ORDER

The wide range of historical documents now to be found on the net concerning all aspects of law and order make interesting reading. Here are just some of the thousands of resources, including those dealing with convicts who were sent to the colonies when transportation was seen both as a means of ridding Britain of its criminal classes and as a sure way to populate newly claimed lands. Contrary to popular opinion, transportation was not in itself a statutory punishment but was in most cases, at least initially, an option given to a prisoner who had been sentenced to death. Records of these and other criminals are constantly being gathered by individuals, commercial sites and family history societies and many are already available online.

STATUTE & COMMON LAW

http://www.statutelaw.gov.uk/Home.aspx (UK Statute Law Database – search here for any law throughout history by name, date or type)
http://www.medievalgenealogy.org.uk/guide/leg.shtml (Guide to miscellaneous branches of Common Law with links)

ASSIZE RECORDS

http://www.british-history.ac.uk/catalogue.asp?gid=50 (British History Online website for searching Assize records)
http://www.nationalarchives.gov.uk/catalogue/Leaflets/ri2231.htm (National Archives' guide to researching Assize records with links)

QUARTER SESSIONS RECORDS

http://www.genuki.org.uk/search/ (Enter the words 'Quarter Sessions' into the search engine on this page to access nearly a thousand references countrywide)
http://www.gmcro.co.uk/cs/quarter_sessions.htm (General explanation of using Quarter Sessions records for family history)
http://www.lynherparishes.co.uk/General/QuarterSessions.htm (List of some records held by the Cornwall Record Office)

COURT OF CHANCERY

http://www.medievalgenealogy.org.uk/guide/cha.shtml (Guide to using British Court of Chancery records plus links; disputes over debts, inheritance, land, etc from the 14th century to 19th century)
http://www.ancestry.co.uk/search/db.aspx?dbid=7919 (Search Chancery records 1386-1558; subscription site)
http://www.originsnetwork.com/help/popup-aboutbo-indis.htm (Inheritance Disputes Index 1574-1714 of cases from the Court of Chancery – subscription required)
http://www.nas.gov.uk/guides/chancery.asp (Guide to Scottish Chancery records)

CLOSE ROLLS

http://www.stradling.org.uk/docs/Cclr.htm (An explanation of the use of Close Rolls – concerning deeds, conveyances, etc from the 13th century – for family history with examples)

INQUISITIONS POST-MORTEM

http://www.british-history.ac.uk/report.asp?compid=48091 (Page of explanation of Inquisitions Post-Mortem 13th century to 17th century – enquiries made after the death of a Crown landholder – with additional pages containing transcripts of early IPMs)

PATENT ROLLS (LETTERS PATENT)

http://sdrc.lib.uiowa.edu/patentrolls/search.html (Browse or search British Patent Rolls – or Letters Patent – from 1216-1452; concerned the granting of rights and privileges)

COURT OF KING'S BENCH

http://www.british-history.ac.uk/search.asp?query1=%22king%27s+bench%22 (Links to pages concerning King's Bench records, 12th to 19th centuries, which settled disputes when Crown property was involved)

COURT OF REQUESTS

http://www.nationalarchives.gov.uk/familyhistory/guide/ancestorslaw/court.htm (Explanation and records links regarding the Court of Requests 1483-1642, land and financial disputes)

COURT OF STAR CHAMBER

http://www.british-history.ac.uk/report.asp?compid=48094 (Explanation of the court proceedings of the Star Chamber, with links)

COURT OF WARDS & LIVERIES

http://www.nationalarchives.gov.uk/catalogue/Leaflets/ri2229.htm (Details of the Court of Wards and Liveries, from the 1540s and concerned with land inheritance, with links to documents available)
http://www.aim25.ac.uk/cgi-bin/search2?coll_id=3205&inst_id=14 (Records of the Court of Wards and Liveries at the Senate House Library, London and access details)

EYRES

http://www.british-history.ac.uk/subject.asp?subject=1&gid=49 (Records of Eyres and other administrative/legal history)
http://www.british-history.ac.uk/search.asp?query1=london+eyre (Links to records and information)

COURT RECORDS & FINES (GENERAL)

http://www.nationalarchives.gov.uk/search/quick_search.aspx?search_text=court (Law and order resources at The National Archives)
http://www.scotlandspeople.gov.uk/content/help/index.aspx?r=551&565 (About the Scottish court system with links to records useful to family historians)
http://www.wirksworth.org.uk/CRIME.htm (Crime records in Derbyshire 1770-1828)

http://www.originsnetwork.com/help/popup-aboutbo-lccd.htm (Indexes of London Consistory Courts – subscription site)

http://www.nas.gov.uk/guides/sheriffCourt.asp (Scottish Sheriff Court records)

http://www.nottinghamshire.gov.uk/home/leisure/archives/archivescollections/archivescourt.htm (Nottinghamshire court records)

http://www.scan.org.uk/researchrtools/courtrecords.htm (Samples of miscellaneous court records)

http://www.victorianlondon.org/legal/dickens-lawcourts.htm (Detailed study of Victorian London courts)

OLD BAILEY

http://www.oldbaileyonline.org/search/name/ (Search London's Old Bailey court records, currently 1674-1834)

http://yourarchives.nationalarchives.gov.uk/index.php?title=Old_Bailey_Records_in_the_Corporation_of_London_Record_Office (Records in the Corporation of London Record Office)

CRIMINALS

http://www.genuki.org.uk/search/ (Enter the word 'crime' or 'criminal')

http://www.exclassics.com/newgate/ngintro.htm (Links to lists of criminals under various criminal headings)

http://www.reivers.com/namest.htm (List of surnames of Northumberland and Borders sheep stealers)

http://freespace.virgin.net/genealogical.collections/NaughtyFolk.htm (Some Wiltshire criminal records 1864-1855)

http://www.genuki.org.uk/big/eng/GLS/Thornbury/PoachingAffray.html (List of poachers in Gloucester Gaol in 1816)

http://www.genuki.org.uk/big/wal/WelshMurders.html (Welsh murders 1770-1918)

OUTLAWS & HIGHWAYMEN

http://www.british-history.ac.uk/search.asp?query1=outlaw (Historic references and documents regarding outlawed people)

http://www.outlawsandhighwaymen.com/history.htm (History of outlaws and highwaymen)

http://www.british-history.ac.uk/search.asp?query1=HIGHWAYMAN (Historic documents and references regarding highwaymen)

PARDONS & CLEMENCY PLEAS

http://www.nationalarchives.gov.uk/familyhistory/guide/ancestorslaw/licences.htm (Guide to licences, pardons and clemency plea files in The National Archives) http://www.scfhs.org.uk/scfhs/articles/pardon.html (Cheshire convicts granted pardons in the mid 1800s)

PRISONS & CONVICTS

http://www.genuki.org.uk/search/ (Enter the words 'prisoners' and 'gaol' into this search engine to access over 800 resources regarding UK and Irish prisoners)
http://www.institutions.org.uk/prisons/ (Website devoted to historical prisons)
http://www.fred.net/jefalvey/newgate.html (Newgate Prison page with link to prisoners held there)
http://www.exclassics.com/newgate/ngintro.htm (The Newgate Calendar (to 1842) with lists of criminals under various headings)

TRANSPORTATION

http://members.iinet.com.au/~perthdps/convicts/index.html (A guide to researching transported convicts)
http://www.convictcentral.com/ (Large database specifically aimed at researching transported convict ancestors)
http://users.bigpond.net.au/convicts/ (Resources concerning convicts sent to Australia)
http://cedir.uow.edu.au/programs/FirstFleet/search.html (Database of all the 780 convicts on the First Fleet to Australia but no crew or marines)
http://www.records.nsw.gov.au/archives/convicts_3689.asp (New South Wales government site that allows searching for convicts' names and documents relating to them)
http://members.pcug.org.au/~ppmay/cgi-bin/db/search.cgi (Search for Irish convicts transported to New South Wales)
http://members.pcug.org.au/~ppmay/austlinks.htm (Links to sites in Australia that specialise in convict research)
http://home.vicnet.net.au/%7Edcginc/frames.htm#top (Descendants of convicts' website with 'Members Convict' link to lists of men and women sent to Australia)
http://homepages.ihug.co.nz/~tonyf/parkhurstboys/convicts4.html (Parkhurst prisoners sent to New Zealand)

PUNISHMENTS

http://www.fred.net/jefalvey/execute.html (List of executions in England from 1606 onwards)
http://history.powys.org.uk/history/common/crimenu.html (A look at how offenders were punished in Wales)
http://www.llgc.org.uk/sesiwn_fawr/index_s.htm (Crime and punishment database search)
http://www.smr.herefordshire.gov.uk/education/tudor/tudor%20crime%20and%20punishment.htm (Crime and punishment in Tudor times)

http://www.genuki.org.uk/big/eng/DUR/D_Executions.html (Executions at Durham, 1732-1909)

http://www.stirling.gov.uk/index/stirling/historytimeline.htm?id=112600 (Short list of executions in Stirling 1773-1843)

http://www.alba-gen.co.uk/articles/executepdf.pdf (Executions in England 1606-1895 – PDF file)

http://www.murderfile.net/index2.htm (Executions in the UK – search by year, name or victim 1900-1959 with links to other areas and criminal data)

REFORM SCHOOLS, INDUSTRIAL SCHOOLS & BORSTALS

http://www.institutions.org.uk/reformatories/index.html (Countrywide and county by county list of reformatories and industrial schools in Britain plus staff and other records)

http://www.institutions.org.uk/reformatories/index.html (Reformatories and Industrial Schools web page)

http://homepage.ntlworld.com/jeffery.knaggs/l2386a.html (List of those at the Convent of the Good Shepherd Reformatory School for Girls, Bristol 1901)

WITCH TRIALS

http://www.genuki.org.uk/search/ (Type the word 'witch' into this Genuki search engine to access over 60 references and sources regarding witches in the UK and Ireland)

http://www.british-history.ac.uk/search.asp?query1=witchcraft (Historic references to witches, witchcraft trials and official documents)

http://www.hulford.co.uk/essex.html (Essex witchcraft trials with associated information – search facility)

http://www.hulford.co.uk/trials.html (English witch trials with search)

http://www.gippeswic.demon.co.uk/Persecution.html (East Anglian witch trials site with list of witches)

http://www.lowestoftwitches.com/ (Lowestoft witch trial website)

http://www.pendlewitches.co.uk/ (All about the Pendle, Lancashire witches)

http://www.arts.ed.ac.uk/scothist/courses/eurowitchhunt/ (Edinburgh University site – the European Witch Hunt)

http://www.earlymodernweb.org.uk/emn/index.php/archives/2004/10/from-the-dnb-the-last-convicted-witch-in-england/ (The last convicted witch in England with links to other pages)

LOCAL HISTORY SOCIETIES & GROUPS

Local history and family history often go hand in hand and for those who want to find out more about the way an ancestor lived, joining a local history society is often the quickest way to meet like-minded and knowledgeable individuals.

http://www.local-history.co.uk/Groups/ (Lists of national and regional local history societies)
http://www.balh.co.uk/index.php (Website of the British Association for Local History)

MANORIAL RECORDS

Manorial records – which may be as recent as the early 20th century in some areas – include such documents as court rolls, surveys, maps, terriers, and all other documents relating to the boundaries, franchises, wastes, customs or courts of a manor. Some may still be found locally but the best central source for British records is The National Archives.

http://www.nationalarchives.gov.uk/mdr/ (The National Archives Manorial Documents Register site)
http://www.medievalgenealogy.org.uk/sources/manorial.shtml (Links to various manorial records)
http://www.hull.ac.uk/arc/text_only/collection/manor.html (Manorial records listed by county)
http://www.lancs.ac.uk/depts/history/research/manorial_records.htm (The Cumbrian manorial records project)
http://www.gov.im/mnh/heritage/library/publicinfo/manorial.xml (Isle of Man records)
http://www.isle-of-man.com/manxnotebook/fulltext/manroll/ (Manorial rolls of Isle of Man translated from Latin)
http://www.genuki.org.uk/big/#Manors (Miscellaneous manorial links plus other records)

MAPS & GAZETTEERS

Using old maps and gazetteers is an important aid for anyone researching their family tree, whether it is for locating towns and villages, finding the site of an ancestral home or tracking down an old inn, cemetery or street name. Because of the constant changes to town and county boundaries and place-names, not to mention the demolition of whole streets of buildings and the erection of others on former country fields and waste sites, maps are often essential in understanding the past and its relationship to present times.

GENERAL MAP RESOURCES

http://www.yourbooksonline.co.uk/amember/links.html (Links to online map resources)
http://www.genuki.org.uk/big/eng/Maps.html (Links to old map resources throughout Britain)

http://www.old-maps.co.uk/IndexMapPage2.aspx (Search for old maps and order copies)

http://contueor.com/baedeker/great_britain/ihttp://www.yourmapsonline.org.uk/ (Online old maps and etchings worldwide)

http://www.old-maps.co.uk/ (Commercial site – look for and purchase old maps)

http://www.visionofbritain.org.uk/maps/index.jsp (Historic British map resource 1801-2001)

http://www.hipkiss.org/data/maps.html (Links to online viewable old maps)

http://www.antique-maps-online.co.uk/ (Online antique maps)

http://www.hipkiss.org/data/links.html (Links to old maps and charts)

http://www.leitrim-roscommon.com/heraldry/heraldry.html (Website with an interesting map of Ireland as it was in medieval times c1300)

http://freepages.genealogy.rootsweb.com/~genmaps/index.html (Search here for an old map of any area in England, Scotland or Wales)

COUNTY, LOCAL & REGIONAL MAPS

http://www.genuki.org.uk/big/Britain.html (Counties of England, Wales and Scotland prior to the 1974 Boundary Changes)

http://www.genuki.org.uk/search/ (Type 'parish map' into the search engine on this page to find thousands of links and references to parish maps throughout the UK and Ireland)

http://www.gazetteer.co.uk/gazmap1.htm (Map showing old counties of Britain)

http://www.gazetteer.co.uk/gazmap2.htm (Map of modern British county and unitary administrative authorities)

http://www.yourmapsonline.org.uk/index.htm (Maps listed by county – fees payable)

http://www.england-in-particular.info/parishmaps/m-boundary.html (All about parish boundaries)

http://users.bathspa.ac.uk/greenwood/lplaces.html (Online maps of old London)

http://www.geog.port.ac.uk/webmap/hantsmap/hantsmap/hantsmap.htm (Old Hampshire maps)

http://www.lancscc.gov.uk/environment/oldmap/index.asp (Online old maps of Lancashire)

http://www.sierratel.com/colinf/genuki/cav/Maps/Historical.html (Online Irish maps)

http://www.genuki.org.uk/big/eng/YKS/Misc/Maps/YKSmap.html (Download a detailed map of Yorkshire)

http://www.genuki.org.uk/big/sct/sct_cmap.html (County map of Scotland)

FIELD MAPS

http://www.burtonbradstock.org.uk/History/Old%20Maps/Field%20Names.htm (Example of a map showing field names)

MODERN MAPS, STREETFINDERS etc

http://www.streetmap.co.uk/home.html (Displays maps of modern streets and places – search by name, postcode or grid reference)
http://www.multimap.com/index.htm (Modern map finder)
http://www.streetmap.co.uk/ (Modern street map finder)
http://maps.google.co.uk/ (Google maps – find places and streets as well as towns)

ORDNANCE SURVEY MAPS

http://www.ordnancesurvey.co.uk/oswebsite/ (Website of the Ordnance Survey)
http://www.alangodfreymaps.co.uk/ (Find reprints of old UK Ordnance Survey maps)
http://www.british-history.ac.uk/map.asp (Search for old Ordnance Survey maps using online gazetteer search facility)

SATELLITE MAPS

http://earth.google.com/ (Download 'Google Earth' free and use satellite images to locate countries, places and street locations or even to zoom in on your own house)

SEA AREAS

http://www.stvincent.ac.uk/Resources/Weather/Links/marine.html (Site with map of sea areas around Britain)

GAZETTEERS

http://www.alexandria.ucsb.edu/gazetteer/dgie/DGIE_website/gaz_links.htm (Lists of useful gazetteers covering the world)
http://www.gazetteer.co.uk/section1.htm (Gazetteer of over 50,000 British place-names)
http://www.geo.ed.ac.uk/scotgaz/ (Scottish gazetteer)
http://www.history.ac.uk/cmh/gaz/gazweb2.html (Gazetteer of Markets and Fairs in England and Wales up to 1516)
http://www.british-history.ac.uk/source.asp?pubid=8 (Historical Gazetteer of London before the Great Fire 1666)
http://intarch.ac.uk/journal/issue3/snyder_index.html (Gazetteer of sub-Roman Britain)
http://www.census.gov/cgi-bin/gazetteer (US place-name search and gazetteer)

MEDIEVAL GENEALOGY

It is only the lucky few who can trace their families back to medieval times, often to a well known or aristocratic family. There are, however, a number of websites that can assist researchers in this field.

http://www.medievalgenealogy.org.uk/ (A general guide to families and resources for this period)

http://fmg.ac/ (Foundation for Medieval Genealogy site, for promoting and studying this period)

http://www.rootsweb.com/~medieval/resource.htm (Links to medieval genealogy resources)

http://genforum.genealogy.com/medieval/ (A forum for those with medieval family history interests)

http://freepages.genealogy.rootsweb.com/~tapperofamily/abbrev.html (List of abbreviations used in medieval genealogy)

http://www.castles.me.uk/medieval-occupations.htm (Occupations in medieval times)

http://www.smr.herefordshire.gov.uk/education/medieval_village2.htm (Medieval villages)

http://www.medievalgenealogy.org.uk/sources/brasses1.shtml (Links to monumental brasses on the internet)

http://www.history.ac.uk/cmh/exchequer.html (Medieval Exchequer records guide)

http://www.domesdaybook.co.uk/ (Online Domesday Book with search facility)

http://www.fordham.edu/halsall/source/domesday1.html (All about the Domesday survey)

http://www.middle-ages.org.uk/medieval-london-guilds.htm (All about Medieval Guilds)

http://www.medievalgenealogy.org.uk/cal/medcal.shtml (A medieval calendar)

http://www.leitrim-roscommon.com/heraldry/heraldry.html (Old Irish Heraldry website with an interesting map of Ireland as it was in medieval times c1300)

NEWSPAPER & MAGAZINE RESOURCES

Most newspapers hold archives going back to their first edition, though not all are available to the public. Access to a growing number is now available via the internet, both as free and paid services. The digital index to *The Times* may be available through your local library or record office. Some sites also require users to register and obtain a password. The following is just a small selection, others can be obtained by typing the newspaper or periodical's name into a search engine.

http://www.genuki.org.uk/search/ (Enter 'newspapers' in the search field to access over 1,300 separate old newspaper resources countrywide)

http://www.bodley.ox.ac.uk/ilej/ (Free searchable library of early journals)

http://www.bl.uk/collections/victoria.html (Illustrated newspapers and journals in the British Library, searchable by name)

http://www.thepaperboy.com/ (One of the world's leading sites for finding newspapers around the world)

http://www.bl.uk/collections/newspapers.html (How to gain access to the British Library newspaper collection) http://archive.scotsman.com/ (*The Scotsman* digital archive)

http://www.swansea.gov.uk/index.cfm?articleid=5673 (Search the index of the first Welsh, English-language newspaper 1804-1930)

http://www.old-liverpool.co.uk/ (A collection of items from Liverpool newspapers including Births, Marriages and Deaths)

http://guardian.chadwyck.co.uk/password (Archives of the *Guardian* and the *Observer*)

http://www.neukol.org.uk/tvco/index.php/TVNA_Home (*North East Daily Gazette* archives 1888 with more to be added)

http://freepages.genealogy.rootsweb.com/~mrawson/newspaper2.html (*Kentish Express & Ashford News* entries 1882)

http://www.genuki.org.uk/big/eng/YKS/Misc/Transcriptions/NRY/MaltonMessenger 1856BDM.html (Transcriptions of Births, Marriages and Deaths from the Yorkshire *Malton Messenger* in 1856)

http://www.bodley.ox.ac.uk/ilej/ (Digital library of early journals)

http://www.history.rochester.edu/pennymag/ (Read early editions of the *Penny Magazine* 1832-1835 online)

http://www.origins.org.uk/genuki/NFK/norfolk/newspapers/extracts.shtml (Transcribed extracts from Norfolk newspapers)

http://www.lynherparishes.co.uk/General/Newspaper/NewspaperExtracts.htm (Some Cornish newspaper extracts 1773-1862)

NOBILITY & ARISTOCRACY

If you think or know that you are descended from aristocratic or even royal stock, then there is a possibility that you may be able to trace your lineage further back than most. Here are a few sites that could assist you in your researches. See also under **COATS OF ARMS**.

http://www3.dcs.hull.ac.uk/genealogy/royal/ (British Royal Family genealogical information with its links to other royalty worldwide)

http://www3.dcs.hull.ac.uk/genealogy/ (Links concerning genealogical connections with nobility, aristocrats and royalty, including foreign royals)

http://thepeerage.com/ (Genealogical matters relating to the peerage of Britain including a discussion group)

http://www.burkes-peerage.net/welcome.aspx (Search *Burke's Peerage and Gentry* for the nobility)

http://www.rootsweb.com/~jfuller/gen_mail_nobility.html (International genealogy resources for the nobility)

http://www.hereditarytitles.com/ (Site dedicated to hereditary titles of the British Empire)

OCCUPATIONS

Our family history research is undeniably enhanced by finding out about the occupations of our forebears. Knowing about their trades, what they did and where they worked can add understanding and interest to our knowledge of their past. There are now lots of lists, large and small, on the internet that concentrate on individual trades and occupations, often with valuable supplementary information. See also **DIRECTORIES**.

ALL OCCUPATIONS

http://www.genuki.org.uk/search/ (Type 'occupations' to search over 2,000 internet resources dealing with various trades and jobs; also search for individual occupations)
http://rmhh.co.uk/occup/ (Select occupations by starting letter)
http://www2.warwick.ac.uk/services/library/mrc/catalogues/unions/ (Alphabetical guide to all kinds of trade union records)
http://www.wcml.org.uk/ (The Working Class Movement Library with links and resources)
http://www.genuki.org.uk/big/Occupations.html (Selection of Genuki occupational links)
http://www.rootsweb.com/~jfuller/gen_mail_occ.html (Occupation links listed in alphabetical order)
http://www.bl.uk/collections/oiocfamilyhistory/familyoccupations2.html (British Library listings)
http://en.wikipedia.org/wiki/List_of_occupations (Old and present occupations in alphabetical order)
http://www.scotsfamily.com/occupations.htm (Scottish occupations)
http://www.usgenweb.org/research/occupations.shtml (US site listing occupations)
http://www.castles.me.uk/medieval-occupations.htm (Medieval occupations)
http://www2.warwick.ac.uk/services/library/mrc/subject_guides/family_history/ (Trade records for family historians by category with links to other records)
http://www.cityoflondon.gov.uk/Corporation/leisure_heritage/livery/linklist.htm (Alphabetical list of London Livery Companies)
http://homepages.rootsweb.com/~sam/occupation.html (Occupations found in the Colonies)
http://www.movinghere.org.uk/galleries/roots/caribbean/occupations/occupations.htm (Information with links on recruitment of Caribbean men to UK civil service posts, Merchant Navy, military etc)
http://homepages.rootsweb.com/~george/oldgermanprofessions.html (German occupations)
http://www.theshipslist.com/ships/passengerlists/french_occupations1873.html (French occupations)
http://www.geocities.com/heartland/pointe/8783/italjobs.html (Translation of Italian occupations)

AGRICULTURE

http://www.genuki.org.uk/search/ (Search here for UK and Ireland agricultural records using the term most appropriate, eg 'drovers' or 'farmers')

http://www.rhc.rdg.ac.uk/webview?webviewinterface=21 (Facility to search files of the Museum of English Rural Life for names, photographs etc)

http://www.bahs.org.uk/ (Website of the British Agricultural History Society)

http://www.genuki.org.uk/big/wal/WelshDrovers.html (Info on Welsh cattle drovers)

http://www.familyhistoryonline.net/database/SomersetDorsetFHSgrowers.shtml (Hemp and flax growers' index – fee payable)

APPRENTICESHIPS & INDENTURES

http://www.genuki.org.uk/search/ (Type the word 'apprenticeship' into this search engine to access over 600 apprenticeship and indenture sources throughout Britain and Ireland)

http://www.gmcro.co.uk/exhibitions/apprentices.htm (Illustrated web page about indentures and apprenticeships)

http://freepages.genealogy.rootsweb.com/~mrawson/brasted2.html (Some early apprenticeship listings from Brasted, Kent)

http://www.originsnetwork.com/help/popup-aboutbo-lonapps.htm (Subscription site - London apprenticeship abstracts 1442-1850)

http://www.genuki.org.uk/big/eng/WAR/deloyd/warwickapps1800.html (A short list of Warwick apprentices)

http://freepages.genealogy.rootsweb.com/~mrawson/app1.html (Maidstone apprentice lists 1694-1734)

ARTISTS

http://myweb.tiscali.co.uk/speel/london/londart.htm (Links to biographies of Victorian artists)

http://www.victorianweb.org/painting/paintingov.html (Information on Victorian painters)

http://witcombe.sbc.edu/ARTHLinks.html (General art history resource site)

BANKERS

http://www.danbyrnes.com.au/merchants/ (Chronologically lists merchants, bankers and related history from earliest times to 2002)

BANKRUPTS

http://www.nationalarchives.gov.uk/familyhistory/guide/ancestorslaw/bankruptcy.htm (How to trace bankrupts through official records and archives)

BLACKSMITHS

http://www.blacksmithscompany.org.uk/Pages/History/History_Incorporation.htm
(Website of the Worshipful Company of Blacksmiths)
http://freepages.genealogy.rootsweb.com/~blacksmiths/ (Database of blacksmiths in Britain organised by county, plus others elsewhere)

BOOK TRADE

http://www.bbti.bham.ac.uk/ (An index of names and brief biographical and trade details of those in England and Wales trading by 1851, with link to a similar Scottish index)

BREWERS

http://www.gtj.org.uk/en/filmitems/29141 (Historic film clips of brewery workers)
http://www.midlandspubs.co.uk/ (Midlands pubs and breweries)
http://www.archiveshub.ac.uk/news/guinness.html (How to access the Guinness Archives)
http://www.archiveshub.ac.uk/apr02.shtml (Scottish Brewing Archive)
http://www.breweriana.co.uk (General site concerning all breweriana subjects)
http://www.breweryhistory.co.uk (Brewery History Society Archive links)

BRICKMAKERS

http://www.davidrcufley.btinternet.co.uk/brkindx.htm (Searchable brickmakers' index)
http://www.hertfordshire-genealogy.co.uk/data/occupations/st-albans-brickmakers/st-albans-brickmakers.htm (Brickmakers of St Albans with info and links)
http://www.hertfordshire-genealogy.co.uk/data/occupations/brickmakers-1851.htm (Hertfordshire brickmakers 1851)
http://www.hertfordshire-genealogy.co.uk/data/topics/t036-leverstock-green-bricks.htm (Brickmakers of Leverstock Green)

BRUSH MAKERS

http://www.brushmakers.com/ (Home Page for the Society of Brushmakers' Descendants)

BUILDERS

http://www.lightage.demon.co.uk/PRESIDENTS.htm (Purchase carte de visite photos of prominent Liverpool builders)

BUTCHERS

http://www.ancestryireland.com/database.php?filename=db_butchersinbelfast1830
(List of Belfast butchers in 1830 – membership required)

http://history.foote-family.com/butchers/ (History of Guernsey butchers)
http://www.british-genealogy.com/forums/showthread.php?t=5364 (Nottingham butchers)

CANALS & WATERWAYS

http://www.thewaterwaystrust.co.uk/museums/archives.shtml (Archive holding the largest collection of inland waterways-related material in the United Kingdom)
http://nwm.org.uk/CollectionsArchives.html (National Waterways Archive with links to other similar archives)
http://www.bargemen.co.uk/ (Website of 'The Barge Men' with links to names etc)
http://freespace.virgin.net/anglers.rest/Canalpeople.htm (Forum for those researching family trees amongst those who lived and worked on canals and waterways)
http://www.canaljunction.com/canal/heritage.htm (Website dedicated to the heritage of the canals of Britain)
http://lists.rootsweb.com/index/other/Occupations/CANAL-PEOPLE.html (Canal people mailing list)
http://www.canalmuseum.org.uk/collection/family-history.htm (Family history tips and links for searching for canal and waterway workers)
http://www.genuki.org.uk/big/eng/STS/Names/WolvCanal.html (Baptisms and marriages of Wolverhampton canal people)
http://www.hertfordshire-genealogy.co.uk/data/census/census1881-bargebuilders.htm (A list of Hertfordshire barge builders in 1881)
http://archiver.rootsweb.com/th/index/ENG-THAMESWATERMEN/ (Message board archives dealing with Thames Watermen)
http://www.hants.gov.uk/navaldockyard/index.htm (Deals with all interests in Naval dockyards, with search facility)
http://www.msurman.freeserve.co.uk/www/pages/Glos%20Strays.htm (Gloucester 'strays' on boats in 1841 census)
http://www.jim-shead.com/waterways/Engindex.html (Index of waterway engineers and surveyors)
http://www.jim-shead.com/waterways/Peopleindex.html (Index of waterway people)
http://www.virtualwaterways.co.uk/home.html (The Virtual Waterways Archive Catalogue)
http://www.bodley.ox.ac.uk/external/rchs/index.html (Website of the Railway and Canal Historical Society
http://www.townsleyb.members.beeb.net/Boatmen/ (Website for ancestors connected with waterways and coastal shipping in Northern England

CHARTERED ACCOUNTANTS

http://www.familytreeconnection.com/resources/ftc366.html (Search the membership list of the Institute of Chartered Accountants in Ireland 1916)
http://www.icaew.co.uk/library/index.cfm?AUB=TB2I_27022 (Institute of Chartered Accountants in England and Wales' library and information service)

CHEMISTS & ALCHEMISTS

http://www.open.ac.uk/ou5/Arts/chemists/ (Biographical database of the British Chemical Community, 1880-1970)
http://www.bshs.org.uk/links/chemistry.html (British Society for the History of Science site with links to chemist and alchemical resources)
http://www.liv.ac.uk/Chemistry/Links/refhistory.html (History of chemistry, links including biographies)

CIRCUS & FAIRGROUND WORKERS

http://www.circusbiography.co.uk/project.html (Website of the Dictionary of British Circus Biography project)
http://www.shef.ac.uk/nfa/ (Website of the National Fairground Archive)
http://www.circushistory.org/ (Website of the Circus Historical Society)
http://users.nwon.com/pauline/Travellers.html (Links and lists relating to showmen, circus and fairground travellers)

CLERGYMEN & MISSIONARIES

http://www.lambethpalacelibrary.org/ (Details of the Church of England Record Centre)
http://www.history.ac.uk/gh/clergy.htm (Guildhall Library Guide - sources for tracing clergy and lay persons)
http://eagle.cch.kcl.ac.uk:8080/cce/ (Search by name, diocese, location or workplace for UK Bishops and clergy)
http://www.theclergydatabase.org.uk/ (Database whose objective is to document the careers of all C of E clergymen between 1540 and 1835)
http://www.british-history.ac.uk/search.asp?query1=clergy (Historical lists and documents relating to the clergy)
http://research.yale.edu:8084/missionperiodicals/ (Missionary Periodicals database)
http://www.vt-fcgs.org/catholic.html (US and Canadian Roman Catholic missionaries)
http://www-sul.stanford.edu/africa/history/missionarymicroforms.html (Guide to sources for African missionaries)
http://www.wheaton.edu/bgc/archives/GUIDES/236.htm (African Mission archives)
http://janus.lib.cam.ac.uk/db/node.xsp?submit=Go&search=missionaries (Search for various missionary records and resources)
http://www.cwmission.org.uk/about/default.cfm?FeatureID=8 (Site related to the former London and Commonwealth Missionary Societies Archives)
http://www.martynmission.cam.ac.uk/ (Henry Martin Centre for the Study of Mission and World Christianity)
http://www.usc.edu/libraries/archives/arc/digarchives/mission/ (Photo archive for both Catholic and Protestant missions)
http://www2.div.ed.ac.uk/other/mms/mmsresearch.htm (Methodist Mission research resources)

http://www.mundus.ac.uk/ (Gateway to missionary collections in the UK)
http://webarchive.cms-uk.org/library.htm (Website of the Church Mission Society with details of how to access records)

CLOCK & WATCH MAKERS

http://www.clockmakers.archivist.info/wiki/wiki.phtml?title=Clock_%26_
Watchmakers (Alphabetical historical lists of clock and watchmakers)
http://www.bhi.co.uk/hj/HJ%20Obituaries.htm (British Horological Institute list of obituaries)
http://lists.rootsweb.com/index/intl/UK/UK-WATCHMAKERS.html (Watchmakers mailing list and archives)

COACHMEN & CARRIERS

http://www.genuki.org.uk/search/ (Type the words 'coaches', 'coachman' and 'carrier' separately into this search engine to get hundreds of links to trade directories)
http://www.hertfordshire-genealogy.co.uk/data/occupations/coaches-inns-
redbourn.htm (Coachmen in Redbourn 1830s)
http://www.british-history.ac.uk/report.asp?compid=43923 (Historic coachman resources)
http://www.anvil.clara.net/stage.htm (A general study of coaching)

COASTGUARDS & CUSTOMS OFFICERS

http://www.ancestryireland.com/database.php?filename=db_coastguardofficers_
1864 (Search for Irish Coastguards – subscription service)
http://www.trinityhouse.co.uk/corporation/genealogy.html (Trinity house genealogy links)
http://www.ukshipregister.co.uk/mcga-hmcg_rescue/mcga-dops_sar_hmcg-
genealogical.htm (Tips on tracing Coastguard ancestors from the UK Maritime & Coastguard Agency)
http://www.hillsd.freeserve.co.uk/marhist/shoreidx.htm (Smuggling site with access to names, including Customs officers, places and ships)
http://www.nationalarchives.gov.uk/catalogue/Leaflets/ri2044.htm (History of the Coastguard service with information about which records to consult)
http://www.nationalarchives.gov.uk/leaflets/ (The National Archives site where you can obtain a leaflet about consulting official records of Coastguards)
http://www.genuki.org.uk/big/Coastguards/index.html (A list of British Coastguards 1841-1901)
http://www.mariners-l.co.uk/UKCustoms.html (Details of official documents available for researching Customs staff)

COBBLERS/BOOT & SHOEMAKERS

http://www.genuki.org.uk/search/ (Type the words 'shoemaker', 'cobbler' or cordwainer' into the search engine)
http://www.genuki.org.uk/big/eng/YKS/Misc/Trades/Boot_shoe_makers_of_Yorkshire2.txt (List of Yorkshire boot and shoe makers)

CUTLERS

http://freepages.history.rootsweb.com/~exy1/fh_material/spring_knife_cutlers.html (List of 19th century Sheffield cutlers)

EAST INDIA COMPANY

http://www.bl.uk/collections/iorgenrl.html (How to access the records of the East India Company and related documentation)
http://www.aigs.org.au/britind.htm (Information and links about the East India Company)
http://youroldbooksandmaps.co.uk/East-India-Registers-p-1-c-52.html (Commercial site selling lists pertaining to the EIC)

DIVERS

http://www.thehds.com/divers/ (Search the Historical Diving Society's database of divers and associated trades)

DOCTORS, PHYSICIANS & MEDICAL SUBJECTS

http://user.itl.net/~glen/doctors.html (Links to resources for tracing doctors and physicians including those in the forces and abroad)
http://library.wellcome.ac.uk/doc_WTL039654.htmll (Medical Archives and Manuscripts Survey list of resources)
http://www.ums.ac.uk/archives.html (Ulster Medical Science Archives website)
http://histsciences.univ-paris1.fr/databases/cpl/ (Irregular Practitioners 1550-1640 database and book)

ENGINEERING AND TECHNOLOGY

http://www.iee.org/TheIEE/Research/Archives/ (Archive collection of material held to promote and preserve the history of engineering and technology)
http://www.ice.org.uk/knowledge/library_heritage.asp (Institute of Civil Engineers heritage page)
http://www.cornucopia.org.uk/html/search/verb/GetRecord/6735 (Clickable links to the Institute of Civil Engineers' library)

FIREMEN

http://www.genuki.org.uk/search/ (Enter 'fireman' and 'firemen' into this Genuki search engine to find over 200 individual sources concerning firemen)
http://www.croatians.com/1aFIREMEN-1855%20LIST.htm (1855-1856 firemen in San Francisco – including immigrants)

FISHERMEN & WHALERS

http://www.genuki.org.uk/search/ (Search the Genuki archives using the words 'fisherman' or 'fishing' to obtain hundreds of genealogical resources throughout the UK and Ireland)
http://www.mariners-l.co.uk/UKFishermen.html (The mariners mailing list – tracing fishermen in British waters)
http://www.mariners-l.co.uk/Grimsbyfishermendeaths.html (Board of Trade list of drowned mariners reported at Grimsby 1878-1872)
http://www.mariners-l.co.uk/Hullfishermendeaths.html (Hull fishermen who died at sea 1878-1882)
http://www.edinphoto.org.uk/0_a_l/0_around_edinburgh_-_newhaven.htm (Old photographs relating to fishermen and fishing)
http://explorenorth.com/whalers/ (Whalers Heritage Project for researching whaling ancestors)
http://explorenorth.com/whalers/ships-whitby.html (List of whale boats sailing from Whitby 1753-1837)
http://explorenorth.com/whalers/whalers.htm (Whalers Index from the Whalers Heritage Project)
http://explorenorth.com/whalers/crew-prospect.html (Crew list of the whaling ship *Prospect*, of Whitby 1788)
http://explorenorth.com/whalers/crew-volunteer.html (Crew lists of the Whaling ship *Volunteer*, 1772 and 1815)

FLESHERS

http://www.fifefhs.org/Records/trades/burntfl.htm (List of Burntisland fleshers – butchers who did not slaughter as part of their profession)

GAS WORKERS

http://www.gasarchive.org/ (National Gas Archive website)
http://www.spartacus.schoolnet.co.uk/TUgas.htm (Website of the National Union of Gasworkers)

GUN MAKERS & ALLIED TRADES

http://www.genuki.org.uk/big/Gunmakers.html (A look-up service from an index of over 9,000 names)
http://www.internetgunclub.com/general/history.php (Search the Internet Gun Club's database of gunmakers)

GYPSY, ROMANY & TRAVELLERS RECORDS

http://www.rtfhs.org.uk/ (Site dedicated to the family history of travelling communities, their employment, history, culture and background)
http://lists.rootsweb.com/index/intl/UK/UK-ROMANI.html (UK- Romany mailing list)
http://users.nwon.com/pauline/Travellers.html (Links and lists relating to showmen, circus and fairground travellers)

HANGMEN & EXECUTIONERS

http://www.richard.clark32.btinternet.co.uk/hangmen.html (English hangmen 1850-1964)
http://executions.mysite.wanadoo-members.co.uk/page2.html (Executions in Ireland by English hangmen with details of those hung)
http://www.real-crime.co.uk/Murder1/HANG1.HTML (Famous hangmen and notable executions)

LAWYERS, ATTORNEYS & SOLICITORS

http://www.lawsociety.org.uk/productsandservices/libraryservices/legalresearchguides/view=article.law?PUBLICATIONID=228200 (Guide to tracing past solicitors)
http://www.innertemple.org.uk/archive/itad/index.asp (The Inner Temple Admissions database)
http://content.ancestry.co.uk/iexec/?htx=List&dbid=8022&offerid=0%3a7858%3a0 (Search the Law List 1843)
http://www.nationalarchives.gov.uk/familyhistory/guide/trade/attorneys.htm (Access to records at The National Archives)

LEATHER WORKERS AND TANNERS

http://www.genuki.org.uk/big/eng/DBY/BygoneIndustries/TannerWorks.html (Web page about the Peak District leather and tanning industry)
http://www.smr.herefordshire.gov.uk/agriculture%20_industry/tanning.htm (Page with maps of tanning establishments in Herefordshire)
http://www.british-history.ac.uk/search.asp?query1=tanner (Historical documents listing one or more tanners)
http://www.walsall.gov.uk/index/leisure_and_culture/leathermuseum/history_

of_leather.htm (The Walsall district leather industry with PDF files listing individual workers)

LIGHTHOUSE KEEPERS

http://www.genuki.org.uk/big/Lighthouses/ (Lighthouse personnel in England, Wales and the Channel Islands c1790-1911)
http://www.history.ac.uk/gh/lhouse.htm (Sources from the Guildhall Library)
http://www.nas.gov.uk/guides/lighthouses.asp (Guide to Scottish lighthouse records)
http://www.originsnetwork.com/help/popup-aboutbo-trinity2.htm (How to search the Trinity House calendars 1787-1854)

LOCKSMITHS

http://www.locksmithsregister.com/history.php (A history of locksmiths, with links)

MARINERS/MERCHANT NAVY

http://www.nmm.ac.uk/server/show/conWebDoc.588/viewPage/2 (Research guide for tracing merchant seamen)
http://www.mcga.gov.uk/c4mca/mcga-seafarer_information/mcga-rss-home.htm (Registry of Shipping and Seamen website)
http://www.genuki.org.uk/big/MerchantMarine.html (Site containing lots of maritime resource links)
http://www.red-duster.co.uk/chart%20room.htm (Merchant navy information and links)
http://www.searcher-na.co.uk/merchant_navy_records.htm (Guide to official records and what you will find in them)
http://www.mna.org.uk/Research.htm (Merchant Navy Association homepage)
http://1881.ships.breccen.com/1881/1881_ship.html (Crews on ships in Wales 1881)
http://www.swanseamariners.org.uk/ (Swansea maritime records including sailors, ships and much more)
http://www.welshmariners.org.uk/ (Welsh mariners and naval database)
http://www.mariners-l.co.uk/UK19thCSeamen.html (Website of the Mariners Mailing List)
http://www.mun.ca/mha/ (Maritime history website based in Canada)
http://archive.liverpool.gov.uk/leaflets/merchantseamen.html (Liverpool guide to tracing Merchant seamen's records)
http://www.societe-jersiaise.org/alexgle/JMSBS.html (Jersey-based Merchant seamen resource site)

MATHEMATICIANS

http://www-groups.dcs.st-and.ac.uk/~history/Davis/index.html (Women in the British Isles, 1878-1940 who graduated as mathematicians – search by name or university)

MERCHANTS

http://www.danbyrnes.com.au/merchants/ (Chronologically lists merchants, bankers and related history from earliest times to 2002)
http://dbwebtest.liv.ac.uk/merchants/ (Liverpool merchants' and ship owners' database)

MILLERS

http://www.millarchive.com/ (Website designed to share records and history relating to traditional mills and milling)
http://www.hertfordshire-genealogy.co.uk/data/projects/bernardsheath/booklet-windmills.htm (Windmills of St Albans in the 1600s and 1700s)

MINERS, MINING & QUARRYING

http://www.genuki.org.uk/search/ (Type the word 'coal' into this Genuki search engine to access almost 4,000 UK and Ireland coal mining resources)
http://www.cmhrc.pwp.blueyonder.co.uk/ (Coal mining resource centre including names of those involved in pit disasters)
http://www.projects.ex.ac.uk/mhn/nmrsintro.htm (Northern mine research society)
http://www.tidza.demon.co.uk/ (Peak District Mines Historical Society)
http://www.welshmines.org/ (Welsh Mines Society)
http://www.welshcoalmines.co.uk/ (Welsh coal mine page with links)
http://lists.rootsweb.com/index/intl/UK/UK-COALMINERS.html (UK coal miners' genealogy mailing list)
http://shropshiremines.org.uk/bmd/bmdref.htm (Mining database - tips and links for researching miners and mining)
http://www.mining-memorabilia.co.uk/ (Website of the National Mining Memorabilia Association)
http://www.dmm.org.uk/mindex.htm (Website of the Durham Mining Museum with lots of links and resources)
http://freepages.genealogy.rootsweb.com/~stonemen/ (Stone and quarry men of the West Country – search facility)
http://www.pznow.co.uk/historic1/tin.html (Information on the tin miners of Cornwall and associated workers)
http://www.bbc.co.uk/nationonfilm/topics/tin-mining/ (BBC Cornish tin mining web page with film clips)

MUSICIANS

http://www.bios.org.uk/ (Website of the British Institute of Organ Studies)
http://www.harrogate.co.uk/harrogate-band/misc25.htm (Brass band genealogy site)
http://www.musicweb-international.com/garlands/alphabetA.htm (Alphabetical index of music composers)

NURSES & MIDWIVES

http://rcnarchive.rcn.org.uk/ (Access to the Royal College of Nursing archives)
http://www.nationalarchives.gov.uk/familyhistory/guide/trade/nurses.htm (How to access registers and rolls of nurses at The National Archives)
http://www.scarletfinders.co.uk/ (Military nursing website)
http://www.ukchnm.org/ (Website of the United Kingdom centre for the history of nursing and midwifery)

PAPERMAKERS

http://www.papermakers.org.uk/ (Growing database of papermakers)
http://www.hertfordshire-genealogy.co.uk/data/answers/answers-2003/ans-0363-hatfield-papermaker.htm (Papermakers of Hatfield)
http://www.hertfordshire-genealogy.co.uk/data/books/books-1/book0136-paper-mills.htm (Extracts from *Paper Mills and Paper Makers in England 1495-1800*)
http://www.hertfordshire-genealogy.co.uk/data/answers/answers-2003/ans-0370-warrell.htm (Early 19th century papermakers)
http://www.genuki.org.uk/big/wal/Paper.html (Welsh papermakers and paper mills 1700-1900)
http://www.fifefhs.org/Photos/Work/paperworkers.htm (Names of Markinch paper workers 1890s with photograph)
http://www.fifefhs.org/Photos/Work/paperworkers2.htm (More Markinch workers from 1930s with photograph)
http://www.fifefhs.org/Photos/Work/inverpapermill.htm (Names of Inverkeithing paper workers with photograph c1930)

PARISH CLERKS, SEXTONS & CHURCHWARDENS

http://steve.pickthall.users.btopenworld.com/pci/4.html (Alphabetical lists of parish clerks located by county)
http://steve.pickthall.users.btopenworld.com/pci/ (Database of parish clerks, sextons, churchwardens etc)
http://www.genuki.org.uk/cgi-bin/htsearch?words=churchwardens&method=and&format=builtin-short&matchesperpage=20&sort=score&config=genuki (If this long address seems daunting simply type the word 'Churchwardens' into the Genuki search page)

PILOTS (MARINE)

http://www.isle-of-wight-fhs.co.uk/cpilot.htm (Cowes, Isle of Wight, pilots list 1808)
http://www.hometown.aol.com/PRode18115/ (Bristol Channel pilots page with other maritime links)

PHOTOGRAPHERS

http://mywebpage.netscape.com/hibchris/instant/aboutme.html (Database of British Victorian photographers 1850-1901 + trade cards, adverts etc)

http://findingphotographers.homestead.com/files/FF-Index.htm (Global resources for finding photographers)

http://www.thornburypump.myby.co.uk/PI/biogs.html (Biographies of individual photographers)

http://www.rogerco.freeserve.co.uk/ (Illustrated website of Victorian and Edwardian photography and photographers)

http://www.rogerco.freeserve.co.uk/victoria.htm (Selective lists of British photographers by location)

http://www.thornburypump.myby.co.uk/PI/index.html (Database to enable the dating of old photographs by photographer's name. There are also biographies of photographers)

http://www.cartes.fsnet.co.uk/photo/azlist2.htm (Lists of photographers operating in Bristol 1852-1972)

http://www.photolondon.org.uk/directory.htm (A directory of London photographers 1841-1908)

http://www.edinphoto.org.uk/2/2__professional_photographers.htm (Lists of Edinburgh photographers from 1839 onwards)

http://www.evidenceincamera.co.uk/ (RAF Aerial Reconnaissance Archives)

http://www.genuki.org.uk/big/wal/AberPhotos.html (Aberystwyth photographers 1857-1900)

http://freepages.genealogy.rootsweb.com/~liverpoolphotographers/ (Directory listings of Liverpool photographers 1860-1930)

http://www.feldgrau.com/wsskb.html (German photographers in World War II)

POETS

http://www.poetsgraves.co.uk/b.htm (Biographies and burial places)

POLICE (CIVIL)

http://www.genuki.org.uk/search/ (Type 'police' into this website to find hundreds of UK and Irish police records)

http://www.nationalarchives.gov.uk/catalogue/RdLeaflet.asp?sLeafletID=104&j=1 (Metropolitan Police records held at The National Archives)

http://www.met.police.uk/history/ (Metropolitan Police site with history, links etc)

http://www.genuki.org.uk/big/Police.html (UK police research resources and links)

http://www.policememorial.org.uk/Information/Family%20History/Family_History.htm (Lots of police history and family history links)

http://www.policehistorysociety.co.uk/ (UK police history site)

http://www.policememorial.org.uk/Home.htm (Rolls of honour of police who died in the course of their duty

http://www.essex.police.uk/memorial/ww1.htm (Essex Police Memorial Trust web site) http://homepage.ntlworld.com/jeffery.knaggs/l0101a.html (List of residents in Police Section House, 82 Charing Cross Road, Westminster in 1901)

http://www.policememorial.org.uk/Information/Family%20History/Family_History.htm (Lots of police history and family history links)

http://www.historybytheyard.co.uk/family_history.htm (London police family history page with useful links)

http://www.nationalarchives.gov.uk/familyhistory/guide/trade/ric.htm (Royal Irish Constabulary resources in The National Archives)

http://www.royalhumanesociety.org.uk/awards/winners/policewinners.htm (List of Royal Humane Society awards won by individual police)

http://www.oldpolicecellsmuseum.org.uk/index.aspx (Police Museum website, Brighton)

http://mail.bris.ac.uk/%7Ehirab/smp2.html (A website researching British members of the Shanghai Municipal Police 1854-1943)

POLICE (TRANSPORT)

http://www.btp.police.uk/History%20Society/History%20Society%20Main.htm (British Transport Police history website with links, includes WWII roll of honour)

POST OFFICE

http://www.postalheritage.org.uk/collections/archive/familyhistory/ (Family history records held by the Post Office plus general G PO research resources)

http://www.postalheritage.org.uk/visiting/related/ (A page on the same site as above with links to other GPO archives and resources)

http://lists.rootsweb.com/index/intl/UK/POSTALWORKERS-UK.html (Postal workers mailing list)

http://www.genuki.org.uk/big/Indexes/POST.txt (Select list of Post Office workers from GPO records)

http://www.postalheritage.org.uk/collections/ (Collections in the British Postal Museum)

http://www.btplc.com/Thegroup/BTsHistory/BTggrouparchives/index.htm (Archives of BT and its predecessors from the early 1800s onwards)

POTTERY WORKERS

http://www.staffs.ac.uk/schools/humanities_and_soc_sciences/resprac2/potbegin.htm (Information on the Potteries in 1840)

http://www.thepotteries.org/allpotters/ (Database of over 1,500 potters located by either name, date or location of factory)

PRISON STAFF (see also LAW & ORDER)

http://www.hertfordshire-genealogy.co.uk/data/census/census1881-prison.htm (List of prison staff at St Albans 1881)

PUBLICANS & INNKEEPERS

http://www.genuki.org.uk/search/ (Type 'publican' or 'innkeeper' separately for access to hundreds of regional records listing these occupations)
http://www.sfowler.force9.co.uk/page_12.htm (Pub history page with links to other sites)
http://www.sfowler.force9.co.uk/page_27.htm (Tips on tracing an ancestor who was a publican or pub worker)
http://www.midlandspubs.co.uk/ (Midlands pubs and breweries)
http://www.archiveshub.ac.uk/news/0608slmia.html (Details of holdings of the Scottish Licences Mutual Insurance Association Ltd, Glasgow)

RAILWAY WORKERS

http://www.railwayancestors.org.uk/ (Railway Ancestors family history society)
http://www.nrm.org.uk/home/home.asp (National Railway Museum site)
http://www.bodley.ox.ac.uk/external/rchs/index.html (Website of the Railway and Canal Historical Society)
http://www.mtholyoke.edu/courses/rschwart/ind_rev/index.html (Background information about the railway industry in the Industrial Revolution including articles and images)
http://www.railwaysarchive.co.uk/genealogy.php (Railways Archives, a non-genealogical site that may answer questions related to your ancestor's employment and lifestyle)
http://www.trap.org.uk/ (Site with resources for tracing railway archives)
http://www.lnwrs.org.uk/ (London and North Western Railway website with lots of resources including staff history databases)
http://www.midlandrailwaystudycentre.org.uk/Staff_detailed.htm (Details of staff and service records held by the Midland Railway Study Centre)

ROYAL HOUSEHOLD EMPLOYEES

http://www.luc.edu/depts/history/bucholz/DCO/ (Database of Royal Court Officers and Servants 1660-1837 – uses PDF files)

SCIENTIFIC INSTRUMENT MAKERS

http://www.adlerplanetarium.org/research/collections/websters/index.shtml (Search the Webster's Instrument Makers database)

SCRIVENERS

http://www.scriveners.org.uk/general.htm (Website of the Worshipful Company of Scriveners)

SERVANTS

http://www.data-archive.ac.uk/findingData/snDescription.asp?sn=2741 (Details of how to access a database of manservants in 1780)

SLAVE WORKERS & FREED MEN

http://www.genuki.org.uk/search/ (Type in the word 'slavery' to access almost 300 research resources)

http://lists.rootsweb.com/index/intl/ENG/ENGLAND-FREEDMEN.html (UK site specialising in slaves and freed men from all ethnic backgrounds including American slaves that came to England)

http://www.scottishexecutive.gov.uk/News/News-Extras/159 (Slavery in Scotland - article, document and transcript)

http://www.liverpoolmuseums.org.uk/ism/ (International Slavery Museum website)

STEAM ENGINE MANUFACTURERS

http://www.geog.port.ac.uk/lifeline/sem_db/sem_db_home.html (Home page of the Steam Engine Makers database)

STRAW INDUSTRY WORKERS

http://www.hertfordshire-genealogy.co.uk/data/occupations/straw-plait-1851.htm (Southern counties straw plait dealers 1851)

http://www.hertfordshire-genealogy.co.uk/data/occupations/straw-plait.htm (Website about the straw plait industry, Hertfordshire)

http://www.hertfordshire-genealogy.co.uk/data/occupations/straw-plait.htm (Information on the straw hat industry with job titles and names of St Albans workers)

http://www.hertfordshire-genealogy.co.uk/data/answers/answers-2001/ans-0135-austin.htm (About straw splitting)

SUGAR REFINERS & BAKERS

http://www.mawer.clara.net/intro.html (A database of some of those involved in the UK sugar refining industry – 16th to 20th centuries)

TALLOW MANUFACTURERS

http://www.hertfordshire-genealogy.co.uk/data/projects/bernardsheath/booklet-tallow-works.htm (Tallow works at Bernard's Heath)

THEATRE & GENERAL ENTERTAINERS

http://freepages.genealogy.rootsweb.com/~jassie/theatre/ (Theatre mailing list with links to other sites)
http://members.tripod.com/FootlightNotes/index.html (Historic biographies, photos and much more from the world of Theatre, and all forms of popular entertainment)
http://math.boisestate.edu/gas/whowaswho/index.htm (D'Oyly Carte Opera Company index of performers 1875-1982.
http://freepages.genealogy.rootsweb.com/~jassie/theatre/ (Theatre UK mailing list)
http://lists.rootsweb.com/index/intl/UK/THEATRE-UK.html (Theatre UK mailing list)
http://www.hissboo.co.uk/musichall_artistes.shtml (Assistance to locate British music hall and variety artists of the past)
http://www.hertfordshire-genealogy.co.uk/data/census/census1881-entertainers.htm (List of Hertfordshire entertainers 1881)
http://www.genealogyreviews.co.uk/enApr07theatre.htm (Commercial site selling a CD "Who's who in the theatre"
http://www.old-liverpool.co.uk/churches.html (Liverpool theatres and playbills)
http://www.bris.ac.uk/theatrecollection/ (Website of the University of Bristol Theatre Collection)
http://www.genuki.org.uk/big/wal/Theatres2.html (Welsh theatres 1844-1870, some personal names mentioned)

TRADE UNION RECORDS

http://www2.warwick.ac.uk/services/library/mrc/catalogues/unions/ (Alphabetical guide to all kinds of trade union records)
http://www.unionancestors.co.uk/ (Trace a union and find out more about it through this website)

UNDERTAKERS

http://www.hertfordshire-genealogy.co.uk/data/topics/t058-undertakers.htm (Short study of undertakers' records)

VETERINARY SURGEONS

http://library.wellcome.ac.uk/doc_WTX023433.html (The Wellcome Collection veterinary database website)
http://www.rvc.ac.uk/AboutUs/Services/Museums/Museum.cfm (Museum of Veterinary History website with search facility)

ORDERS & FRIENDLY SOCIETIES

Membership of Orders and Friendly Societies often played a large part in the lives of our male forebears. These organisations provided regular social activities as well as a means of support for dependents should hard times, injury or death fall upon the breadwinner.

ALL ORDERS

http://www.sfowler.force9.co.uk/page_23.htm (Web page dedicated to Friendly Society research)

http://web.ukonline.co.uk/thursday.handleigh/genealogy/graves/grave-abbreviations.htm (Abbreviations of Orders found on gravestones)

http://www.exonumia.com/art/society.htm (A to Z international list of all fraternal Orders and Societies with links to some of the organisations listed))

http://home.freeuk.net/pastandpresent/chapter_xvi.htm (Armadale Works Friendly Society's page with references to the Free Gardeners, Ancient Shepherds, Rechabites and Freemasons)

BUFFALOES (Royal Antediluvian Order of Buffaloes)

http://raob.org/ (RAOB International website)

http://raob.org/uklodges.htm (UK and Ireland Buffaloes web page with links to individual lodges)

FORESTERS

http://www.foresters.ws/about_us_history.htm (A history of the Order)

FREEMASONS

http://freemasonry.dept.shef.ac.uk/?q=resources_2 (About genealogical records held at the Library and Museum of Freemasonry)

http://www.freemasonry.london.museum/ (Library and Museum of Freemasonry with family history resources)

http://www.grandlodge-england.org/ (Grand Lodge of England website)

http://www.irish-freemasons.org/ (Grand Lodge of Ireland website)

http://www.grandlodgescotland.com/ (Grand Lodge of Scotland website)

http://freemasonry.dept.shef.ac.uk/?q=resources_2 (Centre for Research into Freemasonry including genealogy link)

http://www.jerseymason.org.uk/craft_library.html (Channel Islands Freemasonry)

http://www.grandlodgeoftexas.org/ (American Freemasonry site)

http://www.isle-of-man.com/manxnotebook/history/socs/fmason.htm (A history of Freemasonry and Manx lodges)

GLADES

http://raob.org/glades.htm (Website of the Glades, the female section of the Buffaloes)

KNIGHTS HOSPITALLERS (ORDER OF ST JOHN)

http://www2.prestel.co.uk/church/oosj/history.htm (Website of the Order of St John Knights Hospitallers)

http://www.british-history.ac.uk/search.asp?query1=hospitallers (Links to historical resources concerning the Knights Hospitallers)

KNIGHTS TEMPLARS

http://www.british-history.ac.uk/search.asp?query1=templars (Historical records and resources concerning the Templars)

http://www.compulink.co.uk/~craftings/200years.htm (A history of the Knights Templars)

http://www.rosslyntemplars.org.uk/knights_templar.htm (History of Knights Templars in Scotland)

http://met.open.ac.uk/genuki/big/eng/bkm/Radnage/templars.html (List of Radnage Templars 1237-1557)

http://www.rosslyntemplars.org.uk/index.htm (Website of the Rosslyn Templars)

http://greatprioryofscotland.com/ (Order of the Temple, Scotland)

ODDFELLOWS

http://www.oddfellows.co.uk/history/?page_id=8 (The Oddfellows' home page with various links including contacts)

http://www.isle-of-man.com/manxnotebook/history/socs/oddflws.htm (Web page devoted to the Oddfellows from a Manx point of view)

RECHABITES

http://www.isle-of-man.com/manxnotebook/history/socs/rech_his.htm (A history of the Independent Order of Rechabites with some IOM names)

http://www.british-history.ac.uk/search.asp?query1=rechabites (Historical links to various Rechabite groups)

http://www.isle-of-man.com/manxnotebook/fulltext/rh1911/index.htm (Online book - *A record of the origin, rise and progress of the Independent Order of Rechabites*)

http://genuki.cs.ncl.ac.uk/DEV/Clovelly/Rechabites.html (List of Clovelly Rechabites 1925/6)

http://www.archivesnetworkwales.info/cgi-bin/anw/quicksearch?term=rechabites (Welsh resources)

http://a-day-in-the-life.powys.org.uk/cym/cymdeith/cs_drinkt.php (Brecon Rechabitism)

PARLIAMENTARY & POLITICAL RECORDS

Parliamentary records are useful to family historians whose ancestors have been involved in politics in any way, or have become entangled in affairs where government involvement took place. *Hansard* – the reports of parliamentary proceedings, the Parliamentary archives and the government's oral history collection are accessible from the UK Houses of Parliament website. Mayors and local councillors are often listed on boards in town halls and council offices. A few examples of such lists found on the internet are given below and those for other places can be found using any search engine.

GOVERNMENT / PARLIAMENTARY RECORDS

http://www.parliament.uk/index.cfm (Guide to researching UK Parliament records)
http://www.alba.org.uk/westminster/index.html (Historic lists of Ministers, government officials, election records etc)
http://www.parliament.uk/parliamentary_publications_and_archives/parliamentary_archives.cfm (Parliamentary Archives links)
http://www.histparl.ac.uk/ (History of Parliament including the House of Lords)

CHARTIST MOVEMENT

http://www.chartists.net/ (Website dedicated to the 19th century Chartist movement with links to lists of names etc)

LOCAL POLITICIANS

http://www.origins.org.uk/genuki/NFK/places/n/norwich/mayors_and_sheriffs.shtml (Norwich Mayors, Lord Mayors and Sheriffs 1835-1990)
http://www.genuki.org.uk/big/eng/HUN/MayorsOfHuntingdon.html (Huntingdon Mayors 1800-1840)
http://www.genuki.org.uk/big/eng/NTT/Nottingham/Mayors.html (Nottingham Mayors 1302-1749)
http://freepages.genealogy.rootsweb.com/~mrawson/mayors2.html (Dover Mayors 1606-1665)
http://freepages.genealogy.rootsweb.com/~mrawson/mayors.html (Maidstone Mayors 1649-1721)
http://www.genuki.org.uk/big/eng/YKS/Misc/Transcriptions/WRY/PontefractMayors.html (Pontefract Mayors 1484-1883)
http://www.genuki.org.uk/big/eng/DUR/GatesheadHistory/Ch11.html (Gateshead Mayors 1835-1973)
http://met.open.ac.uk/genuki/big/eng/BKM/Buckingham/bailiffs.html (Buckingham Bailiffs and Mayors 1513-1842)
http://www.genuki.org.uk/big/eng/YKS/Misc/Transcriptions/NRY/ScarboroughBailiffs.html (Scarborough Bailiffs 1600-1810)

http://www.chester.gov.uk/main.asp?page=1065 (Chester Mayors and Sheriffs 1238 -2007)

http://www.wiganworld.co.uk/stuff/wig1889p6.php?opt=wig1889 (Rectors and Mayors of Wigan 1245 -1888)

http://www.lancaster.gov.uk/General.asp?id=SX9452-A7809B16&cat=832 (Mayors of Morecambe and Heysham 1902-1974)

http://www.lancaster.gov.uk/General.asp?id=SX9452-A7807072&cat=832 (Mayors of Lancaster 1498-1937)

http://www.west-norfolk.gov.uk/default.aspx?page=23655 (Mayors of King's Lynn and West Norfolk 1249 to present time)

http://www.british-history.ac.uk/report.asp?compid=45561 (Mayors and Sheriffs of London 1198 – 1470)

MAGNA CARTA

http://www.bl.uk/treasures/magnacarta/translation.html (A translation of King John's agreement with the barony signed in 1215 that was seen at the time as a Bill of Rights for his citizens)

PROTESTATION ROLLS 1641

http://www.genuki.org.uk/search/ (enter the word 'Protestation' into this Genuki search engine to find over 200 resources countrywide)

http://www.dorset-opc.com/ChideockFiles/ChideockProtestation1641.htm (Dorset citizens swearing to defend the Protestant faith of the Civil War period)

http://mpsgg.com/WDIM/WDIM_14.html (Canadian site explaining British Protestation Returns)

INTERREGNUM & CIVIL WAR RECORDS

http://www.british-history.ac.uk/search.asp?query1=interregnum (Official records of the Interregnum and Civil War period)

http://www.british-history.ac.uk/search.asp?query1=civil+war (Specific records dealing with the Civil War in England)

http://www.british-history.ac.uk/search.asp?query1=Royalist+composition+papers (Access to various Royalist Composition records)

OATH OF ALLEGIANCE 1723

http://www.nationalarchives.gov.uk/familyhistory/guide/people/oath.htm (Oath rolls held by The National Archives)

http://www.foda.org.uk/oaths/intro/introduction15.htm (Devon Oath Rolls 1723 with names of those found in them)

PASSPORTS

Passports in the sense that we know them today were not introduced until 1915, but 'safe conduct' certificates were issued in the 15th century and records exist from at least the 18th century for more recent individual documents.

http://www.nationalarchives.gov.uk/catalogue/Leaflets/ri2167.htm (All about using old passport records in The National Archives)
http://www.movinghere.org.uk/galleries/roots/asian/migration/passports.htm (Passport records held at the British Library)
http://www.scan.org.uk/researchrtools/passports.htm (A small selection of old passports to view online)

PHOTOGRAPHY

Though experiments started earlier, the first useful photographs for genealogists were produced in the mid to late 1800s. As well as general historical information, the internet provides expertise and services for the restoration and dating of old prints. A few examples are listed below. See also under **OCCUPATIONS**.

LANTERN SLIDES

http://www.rleggat.com/photohistory/index.html (The Magic Lantern website)

PHOTOGRAPHY - GENERAL

http://www.genuki.org.uk/search/ (Enter the words 'photographs' and 'photographers' separately into the search engine on this page to find over 8,000 photography pages linked to genealogy)
http://www.ted.photographer.org.uk/photohistory_origin.htm (An historic timeline of photographic processes)
http://www.rleggat.com/photohistory/ (A history of photography and photographers up to the 1920s)
http://www.oldukphotos.com/ (Free access website featuring old photographs of the UK)

PHOTOGRAPH DATING

http://www.thornburypump.myby.co.uk/PI/index.html (Database to enable the dating of old photographs by photographer's name. There are also biographies of photographers)
http://www.cartes.freeuk.com/time/date.htm (Tutorial on how to date old photographs)

RESTORATION

http://www.refindtime.co.uk/ (Commercial page offering a photograph restoration and gift service)
http://www.torncorner.com/ (All kinds of photograph restoration and enhancement)
http://www.restoringthepast.co.uk/ (Photograph restoration and image manipulation services)

PLACE-NAMES

The origin of place-names is a fascinating area of study. Some of them relate to people who originally owned the land (eg Harkerside in the Yorkshire Dales, named after the Harker family). It is interesting to discover place-name links to our ancestors, though these are often likely to be found in most cases at a local level, in the names of geographical locations or farms.

ALL PLACES

http://www.genuki.org.uk/search/ (Type 'place names' into this search engine to obtain over 5,000 references to place-name sites and references in Britain and Ireland)
http://www.englishplacenames.co.uk/ (Study of constituent parts of all place-names)
http://www.rampantscotland.com/placenames/placenames1.htm (Scottish place-names around the world)

BRITAIN - GENERAL

http://www.gazetteer.co.uk/ (Gazetteer of British place-names)
http://www.gazetteer.co.uk/gazmap1.htm (Map showing old county names of Britain)
http://www.daelnet.co.uk/placenames/ (Yorkshire place-names)
http://www.catholic-history.org.uk/latin_names.htm (Latin British place-names with modern equivalent)
http://www.countrylovers.co.uk/places/placnams.htm (Place-names and their changes throughout Norse, Anglo-Saxon, Latin and Norman periods of history)
http://www.fatbadgers.co.uk/Britain/places.htm (Changes in place-names throughout British history)

ENGLAND & ENGLISH REGIONS

http://www.nottingham.ac.uk/english/ins/epntest/intro.html (Key to English place-names)
http://cornovia.org.uk/ihpnc/ (Cornish place-names)
http://www.krysstal.com/londname.html (London place-names)
http://www.british-history.ac.uk/source.asp?pubid=3 (Gazetteer of London place-names)
http://www.northeastengland.talktalk.net/Place%20Name%20Meanings%20A%20to%20D.htm (North East England place-names)

http://www.kentarchaeology.org.uk/Research/Libr/KPN/A/01/01.htm (Kent place-names from the 1904-8 Ordnance Survey maps)
http://www.wirksworth.org.uk/DPI.htm (Locate Derbyshire place-names and parishes)
http://www2.prestel.co.uk/aspen/sussex/namelist.html (Sussex place-names)

IRELAND

http://www.n-ireland.co.uk/genealogy/placenames/ (Place-names in Northern Ireland)
http://www.dublin1850.com/general/placenames.html (Meanings of Irish place-names)
http://www.wesleyjohnston.com/users/ireland/geography/placenames.html (Components and evolution of Irish place-names)

ISLE OF MAN

http://www.isle-of-man.com/manxnotebook/fulltext/pn1925/index.htm (Isle of Man place-names)
http://www.feegan.com/manx/placenames.php (Origins and examples of Manx place-names)

SCOTLAND

http://www.st-andrews.ac.uk/institutes/sassi/spns/index.htm (Scottish Place-Name Society)
http://www.luoac.co.uk/other/scottish.php (Scottish place-names and explanations)
http://www.polkadotmittens.co.uk/names/field_names.html (Orkney place and location names)
http://www.shetland-heritage.co.uk/amenitytrust/placenames/placenames.html (Shetland Place-Name Trust website)

WALES

http://www.kc3.co.uk/~bicycle/sideways/welsh.html (Welsh place-names with pronunciation guide)
http://www.croeso-cynnes-wales.co.uk/iaith/meaning.html (North Wales place-name meanings)

PLAQUES, INSCRIPTIONS & DATESTONES

Valuable information can be gleaned from plaques, inscriptions and datestones, but because they are widely distributed most were hard to trace before the internet came on the scene. Below are a few examples of what may be found on the net.

DATESTONES

http://www.societe-jersiaise.org/alexgle/stonejsyofficial.html (Jersey Datestones Register)
http://www.societe-jersiaise.org/alexgle/stonesark.html (Sark datestones)
http://www.angmeringvillage.co.uk/history/datestones.htm (Angmering, Sussex, Village datestones)
http://www.kirkbymalham.info/KMI/kirkbymalham/datestone.html (Kirkby Malham datestones)

INSCRIPTIONS (GENERAL)

http://www.oxfordinscriptions.com/ (Oxford inscriptions on stones and plaques)
http://www.romanbritain.freeserve.co.uk/Rib.htm (Roman inscriptions in Britain)
http://www.roman-britain.org/epigraphy/rib_index.htm (More Romano-British inscriptions)
http://runicdictionary.nottingham.ac.uk/links.php (Links to runic inscriptions)
http://cornwallinscriptions.co.uk/ (Cornwall inscriptions project)

PLAQUES

http://www.aberdeencity.gov.uk/ACCI/web/site/xcp_Plaque.asp (Searchable database of London's Blue Plaques)
http://www.english-heritage.org.uk/server/show/nav.1499 (Information and search facility for the Blue Plaques of London)
http://www.westminster.gov.uk/leisureandculture/greenplaques/ (Westminster's Green Plaque scheme)
http://www.tameside.gov.uk/blueplaque (Thameside Blue Plaques commemorating notable people)
http://www.aberdeencity.gov.uk/ACCI/web/site/xcp_Plaque.asp Commemorative plaques in Aberdeen)
http://www.ulsterhistory.co.uk/plaques.htm (Ulster plaques with biographies)
http://www.manchester2002-uk.com/buildings/blue-plaques.html (Commemorative plaques in Manchester)
http://www.masud.co.uk/ISLAM/bmh/BMH-IRO-blue_plaque.htm (Muslim-related Blue Plaques in London)

REFERENCE INFORMATION

Whether you are searching for an obsolete name, a technical tradesman's term, or require background facts for churches and buildings, the internet can provide for your needs. There are also many free sites providing resources to make your ancestry search much easier and more interesting, including some that will translate foreign language websites into a readable (though not perfect) English form, others that will provide statistical data such as population figures, and those that will make calculations of various sorts.

ABBREVIATIONS

http://www.nationalarchives.gov.uk/documentsonline/help/Abbreviations-rank.asp (Abbreviations found on WWI medal cards)
http://www.sog.org.uk/prc/abbrev.shtml (Abbreviations used in genealogy)
http://www.hgs-online.org.uk/abbreviations.htm (Abbreviations of genealogical organisations and resources)
http://www.genuki.org.uk/big/eng/Indexes/NE_WarDead/Abbreviations.html (Abbreviations found on rolls of honour and war memorials)
http://www.nationalarchives.gov.uk/releases/2006/january/january1/abbreviations.htm (Abbreviations found in Government and Ministerial documents)
http://genuki.cs.ncl.ac.uk/Transcriptions/DUR/CensusAbbrev.html (Abbreviations found in censuses)
http://genuki.cs.ncl.ac.uk/DEV/Churchstanton/AbbrevRP.html (Some abbreviations found in parish records)
http://www.berksfhs.org.uk/compgroup/Talk26Jan2000/abbreviations.htm (Computer jargon abbreviations - useful when consulting some websites)

BUILDINGS

http://www.building-history.pwp.blueyonder.co.uk/ (Lots of resources for researching the history of houses and other buildings)
http://www.astoft.co.uk/arch/index.htm (Architectural styles of old buildings with samples)
http://www.lookingatbuildings.org.uk/default.asp (Looking at old buildings, resources and study aids)

CURRENCY & OLD WEIGHTS & MEASURES

http://measuringworth.com/calculators/ppoweruk/ (Find the historic purchasing power of any amount of money for any date from 1264 to 2006)
http://www.xe.com/ucc/ (Universal modern currency converter)
http://privatewww.essex.ac.uk/~alan/family/N-Units.html (Convert old weights, measures and currency, plus useful list of regnal years)

DICTIONARIES

http://www.s9.com/ (Biographical dictionary – search over 30,000 obituaries of famous and notable people)
http://www.dictionarylink.com/ (Database of links to useful dictionaries of all kinds))

FREE GENEALOGICAL RESOURCES

http://www.genealogy-links.co.uk/html/freebies.html (Free resources for genealogists)
http://www.staffs.ac.uk/schools/humanities_and_soc_sciences/census/vichome.htm (Download free forms for use in your family history research here)

http://www.aston.ac.uk/lis/eis/electronicref.jsp (Links to a wide range of free resources on the net including many useful to family historians)

http://www.genhomepage.com/software.html (A good selection of computer software to aid the tracing of family trees, much of it free)

HANDWRITING, SCRIPTS & PALEOGRAPHY

http://www.ancestry.co.uk/learn/library/article.aspx?article=10375 (Paleography links – how to decipher old handwriting)

http://genealogy.about.com/od/paleography/ (Links to reading, understanding and deciphering old handwritten documents)

http://www.nationalarchives.gov.uk/palaeography/where_to_start.htm (Tips on reading old documents)

LATIN

http://www.genuki.org.uk/search/ (Type 'Latin' into this Genuki search engine to access tutorials, examples and translation resources)

ROMAN NUMERALS

http://www.guernsey.net/~sgibbs/roman.html (Roman numeral and date conversion with online calculator)

http://www.ivtech.com/roman/index.php (A simple online Roman to Arabic or Arabic to Roman numeral converter)

SOCIAL / LOCAL HISTORY

http://www.fachrs.com/ (Family and Community Historical Research Society page)

http://www.bbc.co.uk/history/british/middle_ages/plague_countryside_01.shtml (Effects on populations caused by the plague)

http://booth.lse.ac.uk/ (Charles Booth's searchable online archive of life and labour in London 1886-1903)

http://www.local-history.co.uk/Groups/index.html (List of local history societies in the UK by location)

SURVEYS & STATISTICS

http://www.statistics.gov.uk/ (The Office of National Statistics (ONS) website giving access to government statistics both historical and modern)

http://homepage.ntlworld.com/hitch/gendocs/pop.html (Population statistics charts of Great Britain and Ireland 1570-1931) http://www.genuki.org.uk/big/Gazetteer/Statistics.html (Gazetteer statistics for Britain and Ireland)

TRANSLATION

http://babelfish.altavista.com/ (Translate selected text or a full web page from a foreign language into English – free)
http://www.google.co.uk/language_tools?hl=en (Translation tools from Google)

WAGES

http://www.wirksworth.org.uk/A04VALUE.htm (Resources to locate earnings for various classes of workers from 1264 to 1954)

WAYBACK MACHINE

http://copac.ac.uk/ (A site featuring the Wayback Machine, a search engine designed to find old or extinct websites)

WEATHER

http://www.wirksworth.org.uk/A14WEATH.htm (A brief guide to historical British weather conditions 1600-1900)

RELIGION

It should not be assumed that our ancestors followed the same religion as ourselves and genealogists should always be prepared to check the records of other denominations. Roman Catholic and Church of England records are relatively easy to find and the links below should assist in finding records for some of the lesser known religions and sects, some of which were persecuted from time to time. These events caused large populations to flee and settle in new areas causing many problems when tracing individuals. Amongst these groups were the Huguenots, widely persecuted members of the Protestant Reformed Church of France and adjacent regions in the 16th and 17th centuries. Thousands were killed in Paris during the St Bartholomew's Day Massacre of 1572 and on subsequent occasions. Because Britain was a non Roman Catholic society, many fled here where they settled and gradually became absorbed into British society.

The Quakers, otherwise known as the Society of Friends, began in Britain in the 17th century and gradually spread throughout the world as a peace-loving religious movement without creeds or hierarchical structures. Quaker records are invaluable to researchers as they date from early times and were often quite detailed.

If the religion you are seeking is not listed here, try the websites listed under the

'Nonconformists (General)' subheading below where you will also find Oath Rolls of nonconformists swearing allegiance to the monarch. Also try the Genuki site listed below under the 'All Denominations' heading. See also under **OCCUPATIONS** for clergy, missionaries and church workers and officials.

ALL DENOMINATIONS

http://www.genuki.org.uk/search/ (Search here for records of any denomination in the UK or Ireland)

http://www.mdlp.co.uk/genweb/glossary.htm (Glossary of church terms found in old records)

http://www.ckfswebservices.com/churchdata/search.html (Search for records of all church denominations here)

http://www.hull.ac.uk/oldlib/archives/religion/western.html#monastic (Religious records of all kinds including those at the University of Hull)

http://www.complete-bible-genealogy.com/ (Genealogy of Biblical characters)

http://www.old-liverpool.co.uk/churches.html (Liverpool and Lancashire church and religion links)

BAPTISTS

http://lists.rootsweb.com/index/other/Religion/BAPTIST-CLERGY-N-CHURCHES.html (Baptist clergy links)

http://www.baptisthistory.org.uk/basicpage.php?contents=home&page_title=Home%20Page (Baptist Historical Society page with family history link)

http://www.cyndislist.com/baptist.htm (Worldwide Baptist links)

http://claremontbaptist-shrewsbury.co.uk/history.htm (Potted history of the Claremont Baptist Church)

http://www.rpc.ox.ac.uk/cbhh/Centre.htm (Website for the Centre for Baptist History and Heritage)

BIBLE CHRISTIANS

http://genuki.cs.ncl.ac.uk/DEV/Shebbear/BibleChristians/index.html (Devon resources)

BRETHREN (ALL BRANCHES)

http://www.cob-net.org/docs/groups.htm (Networking site with links to all the different Brethren denominations)

CHURCH BUILDINGS

http://www.genuki.org.uk/big/churchdb/ (Search a database of British churches)

http://www.history.ac.uk/gh/briefs.htm (Guide to historical resources and parish indexes concerning contributions to the rebuilding of St Paul's cathedral c1678)
http://www.genuki.org.uk/search/ (Type 'church' into this search engine to access records, photographs and information from a staggering 40,000 individual web pages)
http://www.churches-uk-ireland.org/ (Search here for pictures and details of the church where your ancestors were baptised, married or buried in Britain or Ireland)
http://www.findachurch.co.uk/home/home.php (UK church directory)

CHURCH OF ENGLAND

http://www.lambethpalacelibrary.org/access/CERC.html (How to use the Church of England Record Centre with links to the Lambeth Palace research facilities)
http://eagle.cch.kcl.ac.uk:8080/cce/ (Searchable database of bishops, ministers and locations)
http://www.lambethpalacelibrary.org/holdings/depositedarchives.html (Holdings of manuscripts and records at Lambeth Palace)

CHURCH OF IRELAND

http://www.ireland.anglican.org/ (Church of Ireland website with a genealogy link)
http://archiver.rootsweb.com/th/index/CHURCHMEN-UK/ (Archives of the Churchmen mailing list)
http://www.british-genealogy.com/resources/books/clergy/ (Book resources for researching clergyman ancestors)

CHURCH OF SCOTLAND

http://www.rootsweb.com/~onpresco/chatham.htm (Transcriptions of Argenteuil records 1820s to 1880s)
http://www.europepresbytery.net/ (Church of Scotland European Presbytery website)
http://www.archiveshub.ac.uk/news/03012302.html (How to access Church of Scotland training college records)

CONGREGATIONAL

http://www.proni.gov.uk/records/private/cr7_1.htm (Irish Congregational resources)
http://www.woodbridgechurch.org.uk/Records/quay/quay.htm (Congregational BMD records, Woodbridge, Suffolk)

CONVENTS

http://homepage.ntlworld.com/jeffery.knaggs/I0109c.html (Residents of St Vincent De Paul's Convent and Orphanage – 9 Lower Seymour Street, Portman Square, Marylebone 1901) http://homepage.ntlworld.com/jeffery.knaggs/I2386a.html (1901 census list of those at Convent of the Good Shepherd and Reformatory School for Girls, Bristol)

HUGUENOTS

http://www.huguenotsociety.org.uk/family/ (Guide to finding Huguenot family records)
http://www.aftc.com.au/Huguenot/Hug.html (List of Huguenot surnames)
http://www.huguenot.netnation.com/general/ (Huguenot Society web page)

JEWS

http://british-jewry.org.uk/ (British Jewry website)
http://www.jeffreymaynard.com/ (Lots of Anglo-Jewish links)
http://www.jewishgen.org/ (JewishGen website with many resources for tracing Jewish ancestry)
http://www.jgsgb.org.uk/ (UK Jewish Genealogical Society)
http://www.jgsny.org/ (U.S.A. Jewish Genealogical Society)
http://www.ajgs.org.au/ (Australian Jewish Genealogical Society)
http://www.jgstoronto.ca/ (Canadian Jewish Genealogical Society)
http://www.nljewgen.org/eng/index.html (Dutch Jewish Genealogy)
http://www.jewishgen.org/ (Worldwide Jewish Genealogy)
http://www.bh.org.il/Genealogy/jewgensocs.aspx (Another worldwide Jewish genealogy site)
http://www.orthohelp.com/geneal/sefpage2.htm (Sephardic and general Jewish genealogy links worldwide)

LUTHERANS

http://www.lutheransonline.com/lutheransonline/genealogy/ (US-based Lutheran genealogy site)

MENNONITES

http://www.mennonite.net/ (Official site of the Mennonite church with congregation search facility)

METHODISTS

http://rylibweb.man.ac.uk/data1/dg/methodist/methguid.html (Guidance in finding and using UK Methodist records)
http://depts.drew.edu/lib/methodist/ (Accessing Methodist records at Drew University USA)
http://rylibweb.man.ac.uk/data1/dg/methodist/bio/bioind.html (Methodist biographical index and archives)

http://rylibweb.man.ac.uk/data1/dg/methodist/ministers/minister.html (List of Methodist circuit ministers)

http://rylibweb.man.ac.uk/data1/dg/methodist/poor/ (Methodism and the poor with link to online old documents viewable online)

MONASTIC RECORDS

http://www.british-history.ac.uk/catalogue.asp?gid=87 (Monastic and cathedral records)

http://yourarchives.nationalarchives.gov.uk/index.php?title=The_Dissolution_of_the_Monasteries_and_Chantries (Web page concentrating on the Dissolution of the Monasteries in Britain and Ireland)

MUSLIM / ISLAM

http://genforum.genealogy.com/muslim/ (Muslim genealogy forum)

http://www.rootsweb.com/~lkawgw/gen267.html (Sri Lanka Muslim genealogy – Jafferjee)

http://www.masud.co.uk/ISLAM/bmh/BMH-IRO-blue_plaque.htm (Muslim Blue Plaques in London)

http://www.ezsoftech.com/akram/prophetslineage.asp (Prophets Lineage website)

http://www.stanford.edu/class/history18n/images/genealogy/ (Genealogy of Muslim Brothers website)

http://link-o-mania.com/main/islamic.htm (Islamic genealogy links)

http://www.rootsweb.com/~mdeastgw/ (Middle East Genweb project)

NONCONFORMISTS (GENERAL)

http://www.cornwall-opc-database.org/searchdb.php?dbname=baptisms_nc (Search for Cornish nonconformists)

http://www.dundeeroots.com/nonconformist.htm (Scottish nonconformist site)

http://www.somerset.gov.uk/archives/NonConfRecs.htm (Sources for nonconformist records in Somerset)

http://www.bedfordshire.gov.uk/CommunityAndLiving/ArchivesAndRecordOffice/Genealogy/Non-ConformistRegisterTranscripts.aspx (Order Bedfordshire nonconformist transcripts here)

http://www.genuki.org.uk/big/eng/LIN/nonconformist.html (Lincolnshire links)

http://www.genuki.bpears.org.uk/NBL/Newcastle/nonconf.html (Newcastle on Tyne resources)

PRESBYTERIANS

http://www.proni.gov.uk/records/private/presindx.htm (Presbyterian records in Ireland)

http://genuki.cs.ncl.ac.uk/DEV/Presbyterians.html (Devon Presbyterians) http://www.europepresbytery.net/ (Church of Scotland European Presbytery website)

QUAKERS

http://www.rootsweb.com/~engqfhs/ (Quaker Family History Society with research links)

http://www.quakerrecords.com/ (Access to a wide variety of Quaker records)

http://www.quaker.org.uk/Templates/Internal.asp?NodeID=90018 (Guide to Quaker genealogical sources)

http://www.leeds.ac.uk/library/spcoll/quaker/quakint1.htm (About the Quaker Archive database at Leeds University Library)

http://www.learndev.hull.ac.uk/quaker/index.cfm?fuseaction=names.home (Search for Quakers by name - Yorkshire Quaker Heritage Project)

http://west-penwith.org.uk/wpenq.htm (West Penwith Quakers)

http://www.gravetext.co.uk/Quaker_Burials/Quaker_Burials_at_Winnows_Hill.pdf (Northumberland Quaker resources including burials – PDF format)

http://www.quakersurnames.net/ (Katie's surname list – a selection of Quaker surname resources)

http://www.rootsweb.com/~quakers/index.htm (American-based Quaker heritage site)

http://www.geocities.com/Heartland/Plains/2064/qresource.htm (US Quaker research facilities)

ROMAN CATHOLICS / RECUSANTS / PAPISTS

http://www.catholic-history.org.uk/cfhs/ (Catholic Family History Society)

http://www.catholic-history.org.uk/crs/records.htm (Index to Catholic records)

http://www.catholic-library.org.uk/ (How to use the resources held by the Catholic Central Library)

http://www.nationalarchives.gov.uk/catalogue/Leaflets/ri2173.htm (The National Archives leaflet on recusant research)

http://www.elizabethan-era.org.uk/elizabethan-recusants-recusancy-laws.htm (All about Elizabethan recusants)

http://www.jacobite.ca/documents/16890320.htm (Scottish proclamation against Papists 1689)

http://history.hanover.edu/texts/ENGref/er87.html (Copy of the Act against recusants of 1593)

http://www.british-history.ac.uk/report.asp?compid=46295 (An act for removing Papists from London 1688)

http://www.catholic-history.org.uk/nwchs/recushandbook.htm (Recusant historian's online handbook)

http://www.users.globalnet.co.uk/~hadland/tvp/tvpcontents.htm (Comprehensive site about the Thames Valley Papists)

http://genuki.cs.ncl.ac.uk/DEV/DevonMisc/Papists.html (List of Papists in Devon 1648)

http://www.genealogy-quest.com/collections/1716-birdforth.html (List of Yorkshire Papists 1716)
http://www.genealogy-quest.com/collections/1716-langbaurgh.html (North Yorkshire Papists 1716)

SWEDENBORGIAN

http://lists.rootsweb.com/index/intl/UK/UK-NEWCHURCH.html (Mailing list and archives for the New (Swedenborgian) Church in the UK)

SHIPPING including PASSENGER & CREW LISTS

Passenger and crew lists can help to plot the movements of people around the world. In the case of sailors it was not uncommon for them to be away from home for one or more years, hopping off one ship when their duties finished and enlisting on another, often in some foreign port. On a smaller scale, crew lists exist of those working on transport vessels and on rivers, canals and waterways. Many are now finding their way on to the internet. Censuses should also be consulted as they list people who are on ships in ports on the night the census was taken. See also **EMIGRATION** and **OCCUPATIONS**.

ALL MARITIME RESOURCES

http://www.theshipslist.com/ (Shipping lists plus passenger and immigration records and other related subjects)
http://www.theshipslist.com/ships/passengerlists/index.htm (Passenger and boat lists, plus other shipping interests)
http://freepages.genealogy.rootsweb.com/~ourstuff/OurPassengerLists.htm (Search for ships by name, then view their passenger lists – or search by port)
http://www.cyndislist.com/ships.htm (Miscellaneous links to passenger lists, shipping, canal, river and waterway research subjects)
http://www.angelfire.com/de/BobSanders/Site.html (Navy and maritime research links and resources)
http://www.pbenyon.plus.com/Naval.html (Lots of Naval and maritime resources)
http://www.mariners-l.co.uk/MarinersList.html (Mariners mailing list)

AUSTRALIA & NEW ZEALAND

http://www.list.jaunay.com/ausnzpassengers/ (Passenger lists to Australia and New Zealand)
http://freepages.genealogy.rootsweb.com/~nzbound/ (Resources for ships and emigrants heading for New Zealand)
http://freepages.genealogy.rootsweb.com/~ourstuff/ (A strange but very useful list of resources for New Zealand)

http://freepages.history.rootsweb.com/~garter1/tobegin.htm (Lists of those on Australia's First Second and Third Fleets)

http://www.nzetc.org/tm/scholarly/tei-McN01Hist-t1-b1-d2.html (Crew of Capt Cook's *Endeavour* 1770)

IRISH & SCOTTISH

http://www.scotlandsclans.com/irshiplists.htm (Irish and Scottish passenger lists)

http://freespace.virgin.net/alan.tupman/sites/irish.htm (Lots of links to Irish passenger sources)

LIVERPOOL DEPARTURES

http://immigrantships.net/departures/lpool.html (Passengers departing from Liverpool 1772-1929)

http://www.old-liverpool.co.uk/captains.html (Liverpool ships, passengers and crew)

PASSENGER & CREW LISTS (INCLUDING LINKS & SEARCHES)

http://distantcousin.com/Links/ships/ (Lots of links to worldwide passenger lists from pre1600s to 1900s)

http://members.aol.com/rprost/passenger.html (Many links to passenger list websites)

http://home.att.net/~wee-monster/onlinelists.html (Large collection of passenger lists and related information)

http://www.cyndislist.com/ships.htm (Links to passenger lists and other maritime sites)

http://rmhh.co.uk/passen.html (Lots of links to passenger and crew lists)

http://www.ancestorsonboard.com/ (Search facility to find passengers using name, ship or port of departure, currently 1890-1929, going to Australia, Canada, India, New Zealand, South Africa and the USA)

http://members.aol.com/rprost/passenger.html (A very useful comprehensive directory of passenger lists on the internet)

http://freespace.virgin.net/alan.tupman/sites/ships.htm (Passenger lists arranged by country and name of ship)

http://www.mayflowerhistory.com/Passengers/passengers.php (Passenger list of the *Mayflower*'s voyage to colonise USA – click names for biographies)

http://www.theshipslist.com/ships/passengerlists/index.htm (Lists of passengers 1700-1900 with various search facilities)

http://shipslists-online.rootschat.net/outbound/ (Passenger lists outbound from Canada and USA)

http://olivetreegenealogy.com/ships/toausp01.shtml (Miscellaneous passenger lists with links to other genealogy subjects)

http://www.passengerlists.co.uk/search.htm (Search for war brides on passenger ships) http://www.canadianwarbrides.com/passenger-lists.asp (War brides bound for Canada on passenger ships)

http://explorenorth.com/whalers/crew-prospect.html (Crew list of the whaling ship *Prospect*, of Whitby 1788)

http://explorenorth.com/whalers/crew-volunteer.html (Crew lists of the whaling ship *Volunteer*, of Whitby 1772 and 1815)

SHIPS

http://www.genuki.org.uk/search/ (Type 'ships' into this search engine for over a thousand resources)

http://www.geocities.com/mppraetorius/ (Palmer's List of Merchant Vessels)

http://www.old-liverpool.co.uk/captains.html (List of Liverpool ships)

http://www.genuki.org.uk/big/Helena.html (Ships and residents of St Helena during Napoleon's imprisonment 1815-1821)

http://homepage.ntlworld.com/jeffery.knaggs/RNShips.html (1901 index of Royal Navy ships and their positions, captains etc at the 1901 census)

http://www.fleetairarmarchive.net/Ships/Index.html (Fleet Air Arm and other shipping links)

http://www.mightyseas.co.uk/ (Lots of links to sailing, steam and other ship resources)

http://www.reach.net/~sc001198/Lloyds.htm (Register of Ships website – search by letter or use provided links)

http://www.lr.org/search?search=research (Researcher information from Lloyd's Register of Shipping)

http://explorenorth.com/whalers/ships-whitby.html (List of Whitby whaling ships 1753-1837)

http://explorenorth.com/whalers/features/whalewrecks.htm (Details of shipwrecked whalers 1746-1907)

http://www.eminorame.karoo.net/shipping1774.htm (Emigrant ships 1774)

http://www.eminorame.karoo.net/shipping1775.htm (Emigrant ships 1775)

http://www.stvincent.ac.uk/Resources/Weather/Links/marine.html (Site with map of sea areas around Britain – useful for pinpointing shipwrecks)

SHIP OWNERS & CAPTAINS

http://dbwebtest.liv.ac.uk/merchants/ (Liverpool merchants and ship owners' database)

http://www.mightyseas.co.uk/marhist/misc/whitehaven_miscellany/owners_masters_1834.htm (Whitehaven ship owners in 1834 with addresses)

http://www.fifefhs.org/Records/kdyshipowners.htm (Some Kirkcaldy ship owners and gravestones)

http://www.genuki.org.uk/big/wal/NevillLlanelly.html (W. H. Nevill and the Llanelly Iron Shipping Company)

http://explorenorth.com/whalers/features/whalecaptains1.htm (List of captains of whale fishing ships)

SHIP BUILDERS & SHIP BREAKERS

http://www.fleetairarmarchive.net/Ships/Shipyards/Shipyards.html (British and worldwide shipyards)

http://www.fleetairarmarchive.net/Ships/Shipyards/Scrapyards.html (Scrapyards and ship breakers resources)

http://www.mariners-l.co.uk/WWIStandardBuilt.htm (WWI ships, shipbuilders and ship types)

SOUTH AFRICA

http://sa-passenger-list.za.net/index.php (Passenger lists and other resources)

TITANIC

http://www.encyclopedia-titanica.org/titanic_passenger_list/ (Passengers and crew of the *Titanic* plus other information about the ship and its voyage)

USA ARRIVALS

http://home.att.net/~wee-monster/passengers.html (Links to sites with lists of passengers arriving in USA)

WELSH SHIPS

http://1881.ships.breccen.com/1881/1881_ship.html (Crews on ships in Wales 1881)

SPORTS & SPORTSMEN

There are literally thousands of websites dedicated to sport. These are just a few that genealogists may find useful.

http://www.genuki.org.uk/search/ (Type the word 'sport' or any individual sport name, such as 'football', to access hundreds of British and Irish sporting documents and resources)

http://www.staffs.ac.uk/schools/humanities_and_soc_sciences/pgstudents/malhen.htm (Sports history website)

http://www.prewarboxing.co.uk/boxers.htm (Database of British boxers who engaged in more than three fights – fee for further details)

http://www.sprig.org.uk/htfo/htfohistory.html (Links to various sporting history resources including documents)

http://www.cricketarchive.co.uk/ (Cricket archive with details of past players, including women, matches etc)

http://www.acscricket.com/ (Facts, figures and statistics about the world of cricket)

http://www.genuki.org.uk/big/eng/DBY/TakeaLook/BullRings.html (Short article about bullfighting in England)
http://www.horseracinghistory.co.uk/hrho/action/viewBrowse?search=Person&type =Trainer (Horse racing archives listing trainers, riders, breeders etc)
http://www.nhrm.co.uk/ (Website of the National Horse Racing Museum)

STRAYS

In genealogical terms, strays are people born or normally living in one place who are found in official records elsewhere, often a census in another town. Many family history societies have compiled lists of strays in their own areas to aid genealogists who are looking for 'missing' members of any particular family.

http://www.ffhs.org.uk/projects/strays.php (The National Strays Index)
http://www.affho.org/projects/strays.php (Strays clearing house - search here for strays)
http://www.genuki.org.uk/big/eng/YKS/Misc/Census/index.html (Yorkshire strays found elsewhere in 1851 and 1881)
http://www.msurman.freeserve.co.uk/www/pages/Glos%20Strays.htm (Gloucester boat people strays)
http://www.wirksworth.org.uk/C51STRY1.htm (Some Derbyshire strays)
http://www.mlfhs.org.uk/AngloScots/ (Page containing database of Scottish strays)
http://strays.morganhold.co.uk/ (Search for strays by place of origin)
http://www.originsnetwork.com/help/helpio-census1841.aspx (Irish strays, 1841 census)

SUPPLIES & SERVICES

Commercial supplies and services are quite easy to find on the net and this is only a small sample of the vast range available at the time of writing.

AUDIO SERVICES

http://www.preciousvoices.co.uk/ (Professional transfer of precious family audio records on tape to CD)

BOOKS & CDs

http://www.samjraymond.btinternet.co.uk/bglg.html (British genealogical library guides)
http://www.gutenberg.org/wiki/Main_Page (A project to transcribe historic books, catalogues and other printed material of all kinds for display online)

http://www.hawgood.co.uk/books.htm (Commercial site with a list of genealogy books for sale)

http://www.my-history.co.uk/acatalog/ (Commercial online listing of books, software etc for family historians)

http://www.genfair.com/shop/system/index.html (Search Genfair's list of books, software and other genealogical resources by area of interest)

http://www.archivecdbooks.org (Commercial company transferring old books, records and directories to CD)

BOOKPLATES

http://www.bookplatesociety.org/ (Website of the Bookplate Society – collections, history, illustrations, buy and sell etc.)

http://www.nls.uk/privatelivesofbooks/bookplates.html (Early bookplates - download free bookplates for your own books)

http://www.corpus.cam.ac.uk/parker/catalogue/bookplates.php (Online illustration of old bookplates)

http://karaart.com/prints/ex-libris/3e.html (Illustrations of early bookplates)

GENEALOGY SOFTWARE & SUPPLIES

http://www.genealogyreviews.co.uk/genealogysoftware.htm (Genealogy software reviews)

http://www.ukgid.com/links/software.html (A selection of computer genealogy programs to purchase)

http://www.genealogyprinters.com/index.php?refid=genealogyprinters2708%20042154 (Charts plus print supplies and services)

http://www.acorns2oaks.info/ (Professional printing of family trees and more)

http://www.GenealogySupplies.com (S & N Genealogy Supplies for mail order books, CDs and software)

MICROFILM / FICHE SUPPLIES

http://www.microfilm.com/ (All microfilm supplies)

http://www.ggbaker.com/Consumables/Consumables.htm (Consumables, services, repairs and parts for microfilm equipment)

http://www.mw-microfilm.co.uk/ (Fiche readers and accessories)

SURNAMES

There are many sites and individual pages dedicated to researching individual surnames or for finding old records that contain a given surname. Some will contain worldwide references; others will have a bias towards, say, English or American families. It is always worth searching all sites regardless of their country of origin as many will refer to foreign national families who originated from Europe. American and Australian sites often contain historical family trees, references and facts that will not be found on British sites. In addition, nearly all the Subjects in this book will also yield surname lists.

ALL SURNAME SEARCHES & LINKS

http://www.surnamenavigator.org/ (Search for a surname using a dozen or so major search engines at once)

http://www.practicalresearchindexes.co.uk/16253/26323/index.html (Search list of names and locations taken from old postcards worldwide – fee payable)

http://www.digiserve.com/heraldry/surnames.htm (Lots of name resources including regional and foreign names)

http://www.ancestry.co.uk/trees/awt/main.aspx (Search 400 million names worldwide)

http://www.daddezio.com/genealogy/search/index.html (Surname search using various search engines)

http://surname.rootschat.com/sit-surnames.php (Search lists by initial letter)

http://www.surnameweb.org/ (General search tool or search by initial letter)

http://www.surnamefinder.com/ (Links to many surname resources)

http://resources.rootsweb.com/surnames/ (Search surnames by initial letter)

http://members.aol.com/infopacrat/main.html (Links to lots of name searches including searches by initial letter)

http://surhelp.rootsweb.com/srchall.html (Help to find surnames worldwide in a wide range of sources)

http://www.relativesremembered.com/searches/advancedsearch.php (Unusual multi-purpose search)

http://rsl.rootsweb.com/cgi-bin/rslsql.cgi (Search Rootsweb archives by name, location and date)

http://resources.rootsweb.com/cgi-bin/metasearch (Multiple site searches)

http://www.dmoz.org/Society/Genealogy/ (Search for any name, address, date, phrase etc on the web)

http://www.searchforancestors.com/quicksearch/ (Index of databases with surname interests)

http://www.worldwidetopsites.com/sites/genealogy.html (Lists specialised surname search engines)

SEARCH LISTS – UK & IRELAND

http://www.genealogy-links.co.uk/html/search.html (Search engine with a British bias)

http://www.county-surnames.co.uk/ (Search surnames by county)

http://www.genuki.org.uk/search/ (Search lots of UK databases for any given name)

http://www.sfhg.org.uk/mipageA.html (Index to burial surnames found in Suffolk)

http://www.nationalarchives.gov.uk/familyhistory/guide/ancestorslaw/name.htm (How to research changes of name in national legal records) http://www.wills4all.netfirms.com/names_in_wills.htm (Growing list of names found in wills throughout Britain)

http://www.quakersurnames.net/ (Katie's surname list – a selection of Quaker surname resources)

http://www.rootsweb.com/~irlkik/ksurnam2.htm (County Kilkenny surname list)

http://www.ukgenealogy.co.uk/ (Search surnames by UK region, plus other resources)

http://www.list.jaunay.com/engnames/ (Online English surnames directory using pre-1947 county divisions)

http://www.ireland.com/ancestor/surname/ (Search for Irish surnames)

http://www.globalgateway.com/features/surnames/index.asp (More Irish name resources)

http://www.goireland.com/genealogy/html/surname_search.htm (Origins of mostly Irish surnames)

http://www.irishroots.com/research.php (Search for Irish surnames)

http://www.reivers.com/namest.htm (Are you descended from a Northumberland or Borders sheep stealing family? – Find out here)

http://www.stevebulman.f9.co.uk/cumbria/jollie_carlisle_f.html (List of Carlisle residents 1811)

http://webs.lanset.com/azazella/cornish_database.html (Cornish databases, transcripts and specific name studies)

http://www.fifefhs.org/Records/Deeds/cupardeeds.htm (Scottish families named in the Cupar Deeds 1716-1862)

SEARCH LISTS - WORLD

http://www.accessgenealogy.com/test/canada.cgi (Canadian surname search)

http://www.accessgenealogy.com/test/oz.cgi (Search for Australian, Tasmanian and New Zealand surnames)

http://www.phlomis.plus.com/c.htm (Search here for a surname with family tree details – international listings)

http://www.aftc.com.au/Huguenot/Hug.html (List of Huguenot surnames)

http://surhelp.rootsweb.com/srchall.html (Search for individual surnames worldwide)

http://members.tripod.com/~Crystal_J/BakerSearch.html (Search in UK, USA, Canada & Germany)

http://www.progenealogists.com/surnamestudy.htm (Distribution of surnames in USA)

http://www.distantcousin.com/Links/surname.html (Surname search with an American bias)

http://surnamesbytown.com/ (World list taking you to a facility to search surnames by individual town in any country)

http://www.geocities.com/Heartland/Estates/5536/index.html (Norwegian surname database)

SURNAME DISTRIBUTION MAPS

http://www.ancestry.com/learn/facts/Fact.aspx?fid=6&ln (Create distribution maps for any surname in the 1891 census, then click to obtain list of entries for that name; pay to view)
http://www.BMDindex.co.uk (Creates maps from 1851 to 2002 as part of the subscription service)

NAME CHANGE RECORDS

http://www.deedpoll.org.uk/ (Details of the process of changing names by Deed Poll)
http://www.nationalarchives.gov.uk/familyhistory/name/default.htm (National Archives' advice on accessing name change records)

ONE NAME WEBSITES

http://www.ffhs.org.uk/members2/onename.php (List of societies that are studying a single surname)
http://www.mycinnamontoast.com/ (Links to other search engines and individual one-name sites)
http://www.one-name.org/ (Guild of One-Name Studies website)

TAXATION

Taxation records, particularly very old ones pertaining to specific areas, can be useful in providing names and locations. Locating them can be difficult, but several websites explain the history and whereabouts of taxation lists.

ALL TAXES

http://www.nationalarchives.gov.uk/search/quick_search.aspx?search_text=Taxes (Links to all tax records held at The National Archives)
http://www.genuki.org.uk/search/ (The Genuki search engine – enter the word 'tax' for thousands of links to old tax documentation sources)
http://www.british-history.ac.uk/search.asp?query1=tax (Search here for historical tax records)
http://www.witheridge-historical-archive.com/taxes.htm (Overview of various ancient taxes)
http://www.medievalgenealogy.org.uk/guide/tax.shtml (Historical guide and links regarding English tax records)
http://www.scan.org.uk/researchrtools/tax.htm (A selection of viewable old tax documents)
http://www.witheridge-historical-archive.com/taxes.htm (Page explaining some early taxes)

HEARTH TAX

http://www.nationalarchives.gov.uk/catalogue/Leaflets/ri2139.htm (All about the Hearth Tax)
http://www.british-history.ac.uk/period.asp?period=7&gid=54 (Sourcing Hearth Tax returns)
http://www.maybole.org/history/Archives/hearthtax1691.htm (Ayrshire Hearth Tax records 1691)
http://www.wirksworth.org.uk/97-HTAX.htm (Wirksworth, Derbyshire Hearth Tax records)
http://edenlinks.rootsweb.com/1gp/RECORDS/HT/HTINDEX.HTM (Hearth Tax payers in Westmorland 1674)

LAND TAX

http://www.uk-genealogy.org.uk/datafiles/landtaxsearch.html (Search returns of Owners of Land in 1873)
http://www.hertfordshire-genealogy.co.uk/data/occupations/land-tax-1863.htm (List of Land Tax commissioners for Hertfordshire in 1863 with source available for other areas)
http://www.bedfordshire.gov.uk/CommunityAndLiving/ArchivesAndRecordOffice/GuidesToCollections/LandTaxRecords.aspx (About Bedfordshire Land Tax records)
http://great-harwood.org.uk/genealogy/babs/Great%20Harwood%20Land%20Tax%201800.htm (Great Harwood Land Tax record with names 1800)
http://www.history.ac.uk/gh/landtax.htm (Land Tax records in the Guildhall Library)
http://genuki.cs.ncl.ac.uk/DEV/Otterton/LandTax1781.html (Land Tax records, Otterton, Devon 1781)

POLL TAX & SUBSIDY ROLLS

http://www.genuki.org.uk/search/ (Type in the word 'subsidy' in the search box to find hundreds of subsidy rolls resources, many with lists of names)
http://www.scotsgenealogy.com/online/info_polltax.htm (Scottish 17th century Poll Tax records, explanatory leaflet)
http://www.genuki.org.uk/big/eng/YKS/Misc/SubsidyRolls/YKS/SubsidyRolls1379Index.html (Subsidy rolls 1379 with lists of names for Yorkshire)
http://www.british-history.ac.uk/report.asp?compid=36016&strquery=clergy (Taxation of the Clergy and Poll Tax 1381)

SCOTTISH TAXES

http://www.nas.gov.uk/guides/taxation.asp (Guide to old Scottish Tax records)
http://www.monikie.org.uk/ah-hearthtax.htm (Extracts from Scottish Hearth Tax records)

WINDOW TAX

http://www.longparish.org.uk/history/windowtax.htm (Short description of the Window Tax 1696-1851)

http://www.headington.org.uk/oxon/people_lists/oxford_1696_window_tax/index.htm (List of Window Tax payers in Oxford, 1696)

http://edenlinks.rootsweb.com/1gp/RECORDS/WIN_TAX_NW.HTM (Window Tax payers in North Westmorland 1777)

http://edenlinks.rootsweb.com/1gp/RECORDS/WIN_TAX_SW.HTM (Window Tax payers in South Westmorland 1777)

VILLAGES

Apart from the task of finding ancestors who lived in particular villages, the genealogist may even have difficulty in tracing the village itself – some have been absorbed by larger conurbations, while others have been abandoned or have shrunk to an extent that they are virtually untraceable or even lost altogether. The internet is particularly useful in tracing these lost villages and in finding maps or other information that will be useful in family tree research. Many present villages have their own community websites so it is always worth searching for them by name on the net.

BRITISH & IRISH VILLAGES

http://www.orion-arts.com/villages/ (Central link for individual village websites)

DESERTED VILLAGES

http://en.wikipedia.org/wiki/List_of_lost_settlements_in_the_UK (List of deserted medieval and shrunken villages)

http://www.hunimex.com/warwick/warks_lost_villages.html (Deserted villages in Warwickshire)

http://www.cotswolds.info/blogs/deserted-villages.shtml (Deserted Cotswold villages)

http://www.bbc.co.uk/history/british/middle_ages/plague_countryside_01.shtml (Villages deserted because of the plague)

http://www.english-heritage.org.uk/server/show/ConProperty.387 (Wharram Percy, Yorkshire deserted village)

LOST VILLAGES

http://www.eng-villages.co.uk/index.html (Site dedicated to the English village with page links to lost villages, village names etc)

http://www.diplomate.freeserve.co.uk/gainsthorpe.htm (Lost Lincolnshire villages)

http://www.smr.herefordshire.gov.uk/education/medieval_village2.htm (Villages lost without trace plus general information on medieval villages)

http://www.abandonedcommunities.co.uk/ (Abandoned Communities website)

MODERN VILLAGES

http://www.ukvillages.co.uk/ (Search here for details of a modern village)

WARTIME & MILITARY RESOURCES

Service records of those who served in the forces are extremely valuable and can provide us with much personal information, even to the extent in some cases of describing the height, eye colour and other features of one of our ancestors. War grave records, regimental sites and those dealing with battles and war history in general are also worth looking at for snippets of information and sometimes anecdotes describing individual soldiers, sailors and air force personnel. An Act of Parliament passed on 6th February 1918, made servicemen over the age of 21 eligible to vote in their home constituency. A few of these lists, known as Absent Voters Lists, can be found online using the link below under World War 1. Civilian and other records are also valuable and appear in abundance on the net. Sample of these are included below together with listings of sites relative to all wars and conflicts that may be of interest to family historians.

ALL GENERAL WARTIME RESOURCES

http://www.familyrelatives.info/#free (List of free wartime resources on the internet)
http://www.veterans-uk.info/ (Veterans Agency website with links to pensions, welfare services, medals etc)
http://www.wartimememories.co.uk/information.html (Wartime Memories Project website)
http://www.armedforces.co.uk/linksserviceorg.htm (A useful website giving links to lots of service organisations, associations and post-conflict support facilities)
http://www.stephen-stratford.co.uk/courts_martial.htm (Unusual website resources including courts martial, military spies and selected regiments)
http://www.britishbattles.com/ (Excellent resource for battles fought by Britain and its Empire forces from the 18th century to the end of the 19th century, illustrated and mapped)
http://www.historyofwar.org/index.html (Online military encyclopaedia of all war subjects)
http://www.mick-gray.co.uk/military_sites.htm (Links to military sites of all kinds)
http://www.wartimesindex.co.uk/ (*The Times* online wartime resources including free surname search – paid membership scheme)
http://www.kcl.ac.uk/iss/archives/about/lhcma.html (Military resources at King's College, London)
http://www.genuki.org.uk/big/MilitaryRecords.html (Online leaflets, links and resources)

http://www.military-genealogy.com/ (Military genealogy specialist website)
http://www.newarkirregulars.org.uk/links/mhresearch.html (Amazingly comprehensive military history site covering the period from ancient times to the 20th century)
http://www.iwm.org.uk/ (All about the Imperial War Museum including family history records)
http://www.rootsweb.com/~rwguide/lesson13.htm (Hints, tips, international links and addresses plus a history of military life in Britain)
http://bubl.ac.uk/Link/m/militaryhistory.htm (Lots of military history links)
http://www.genuki.org.uk/big/MilitaryRecords.html (Genuki's links to military resources)
http://www.old-liverpool.co.uk/Army71.html (Liverpool military families and individuals away from home 1871)
http://www.wargunner.co.uk/index.htm (Lots of wartime stories, links and resources)
http://www.nationalarchives.gov.uk/catalogue/RdLeaflet.asp?sLeafletID=359&j=1 (The National Archives' resources for the armed forces)
http://www.britisharmedforces.org/ns/ns/nat_british_badge_gallery.htm (Resources regarding British armed forces and National Service)
http://www.historyofwar.org/battleframe.html (Timeline of battles throughout history)

ARMY RECORDS

http://www.nationalarchives.gov.uk/catalogue/Leaflets/ri2017.htm (Research references and information regarding British army in The National Archives)
http://www.bl.uk/collections/social/srvlst1b.html (British Army Lists in the British Library)
http://www.national-army-museum.ac.uk/research/ (National Army Museum for researching military career of relative and related subjects)
http://www.genuki.org.uk/big/sct/ (Military genealogy resources – payment required)
http://www.familyrecords.gov.uk/links.htm#military (Official site, links to military and other records)
http://www.genuki.org.uk/big/BritMilRecs.html (Page explaining what records are available when searching for a military ancestor)
http://www.whitgiftdrums.org.uk/order_of_rank.htm (British army ranks and hierarchy explained)
http://www.nationalarchives.gov.uk/catalogue/Leaflets/ri2004.htm (Sources for Officers' records in The National Archives)
http://www.1914-1918.net/grandad/grandad_records.html (A page about obtaining Army Service Records)
http://www.parishchest.com/en-gb/dept_4010.html (British Army Lists available for purchase on CD)
http://homepage.ntlworld.com/jeffery.knaggs/l1100a.html (Soldiers and others at Borden Camp Military Barracks, Headley, Alton, Hampshire in 1901 census)
http://homepage.ntlworld.com/jeffery.knaggs/l0612c.html (Soldiers in Isolation Hospital, Mandora Barracks (Aldershot), Surrey)

http://members.ozemail.com.au/~clday/pensioners.htm (British army pensioners in India 1800-1857)

http://homepage.ntlworld.com/jeffery.knaggs/I0851b.html (List of those in the Beach Rocks Convalescent Home, Sandgate, Kent at the 1901 census)

http://members.ozemail.com.au/~clday/WWI.htm (European recruits in Australian forces during the First World War that were born in India)

http://freepages.genealogy.rootsweb.com/~liverpool/Army71.html (Liverpool military away from home in 1871)

http://www.wirksworth.org.uk/A18-DESR.htm (Detailed list of army deserters 1828-1840 from Derbyshire sources)

http://www.scan.org.uk/researchrtools/military.htm (Miscellaneous military records and transcriptions online)

http://www.redcoat.info/memindex3.htm (Records of officers killed in multiple campaigns)

ARMY DOCKYARD VOLUNTEERS

http://www.genuki.org.uk/big/DockVols.html (List of British Army Dockyard volunteers 1851)

REGIMENTAL INFORMATION

http://www.regiments.org/regiments/#table (Links and resources for every regiment of the Empire and Commonwealth)

http://www.indiaman.com/regiments.htm (British regiments in Asia)

http://www.victoriacross.org.uk/ccregmus.htm (List of Regimental Museums)

http://freepages.genealogy.rootsweb.com/~crossroads/regiments/ (British regiments in Canada and North America prior to 1870, with links)

http://battlefields1418.50megs.com/british_regiments.htm (British regiments in WWI)

http://www.jaunay.com/garrisons.html (British regiments in Australia 1788-1870)

http://users.netconnect.com.au/~ianmac/britain.html (British forces in Victoria, Australia)

http://freepages.history.rootsweb.com/~garter1/tobegin.htm (Australia's British 'Red Coat Regiments' with names)

http://www.roll-of-honour.com/Regiments/ (Regimental rolls of honour links and searches)

http://www.napoleonic-literature.com/Articles/Black_Soldiers.htm (Information regarding black soldiers serving in British regiments in the 19th century)

http://www.geocities.com/Athens/Acropolis/9460/regiment.htm (British regiments in India)

http://www.allempires.com/article/index.php?q=The_Scottish_Highland_Regiments (Scottish regimental information)

http://custermen.com/ItalyWW2/ArmyOrg/BritishOrg.htm (Information regarding British regiments in Italy WWII)

http://battlefieldsww2.50megs.com/normandy_unit_profiles.htm (British regiments in Normandy WWII)

TERRITORIALS

http://www.1914-1918.net/tf.htm (WWI Territorial Forces with links to regiments and divisions)

MILITIA, FENCIBLES, YEOMANRY

http://www.genuki.org.uk/search/ (Genuki search engine - Type in the word 'militia' to access over 700 entries on the subject)

http://www.nationalarchives.gov.uk/familyhistory/guide/army/militia.htm (National Archives' resources regarding militia, volunteers, fencibles and yeomanry)

http://www.fifefhs.org/Records/loyaltay.htm (Lists of names of members of the Loyal Tay Fencibles)

http://www.genuki.org.uk/big/eng/YKS/Misc/Military/Militia1.html (List of officers in North Yorkshire Militia 1758-1907)

http://genuki.cs.ncl.ac.uk/DEV/DevonIndexes/NorthDevonYeomanry.html (Members of the North Devon Yeomanry 1794-1924)

http://www.gmcro.co.uk/sources/militia/milframes.htm (Detailed Militia records in alphabetical order)

http://www.thewardrobe.org.uk/militia.php (Militia resources with search facility)

http://www.proni.gov.uk/records/militia.htm (Irish Militia, yeomanry lists and muster rolls – list of records)

http://www.originsnetwork.com/help/popup-aboutio-militia2.htm (How to use the Militia Attestations index 1872-1915)

http://www.gtj.org.uk/en/themeitems/27029 (Pictures of Welsh Militia uniforms)

ROYAL NAVY & MARINES

http://www.nationalarchives.gov.uk/documentsonline/royal-navy-service.asp (Details of how to search and download details of over 500,000 Royal Navy seamen 1873-1923)

http://www.hants.gov.uk/navaldockyard/index.htm (Naval Dockyard history site with search facilities)

http://homepage.ntlworld.com/jeffery.knaggs/I0732c.html (List of those at Royal Marine Barracks, Chatham, Kent at 1901 census)

http://homepage.ntlworld.com/jeffery.knaggs/I2377a.html (List of those on HMS *Formidable* – training ship, off Portishead, Bristol Channel, at 1901 census)

http://www.pbenyon.plus.com/NZ_Xross_Line/P15.html (Ship's company of HMS *New Zealand* 1919)

http://www.angelfire.com/de/BobSanders/Site.html (Navy and maritime research links and resources) http://www.pbenyon.plus.com/Naval.html (Lots of miscellaneous Naval and maritime resources)

http://www.genuki.org.uk/big/FlgOff1.html (Naval and marine officers listed in the Naval and Military Almanac 1840 A-H)

http://www.genuki.org.uk/big/FlgOff2.html (Naval and marine officers listed in the Naval and Military Almanac 1840 I-Y)

http://homepage.ntlworld.com/jeffery.knaggs/RNShips.html (1901 index of Royal Navy ships and their positions, captains etc)

http://www.nationalarchives.gov.uk/trafalgarancestors/ (Search for ancestors who fought at the battle of Trafalgar)

http://www.fleetairarmarchive.net/Ships/Index.html (WWII aircraft carrier and other Naval shipping links)

ROYAL AIR FORCE & FLEET AIR ARM

http://www.iwm.org.uk/server/show/ConWebDoc.2556 (Information on tracing RAF service records)

http://www.nationalarchives.gov.uk/familyhistory/guide/airforce/default.htm (Guide to Air Force service records in The National Archives)

http://www.raf.mod.uk/history/ (General history of the RAF)

http://www.raf.mod.uk/links/contacts.cfm (Help with tracing Air Force records)

http://www.worldwar2exraf.co.uk/Researching%20Records.html (World War II resources)

http://www.fleetairarmarchive.net/ (The Fleet Air Arm Archives)

http://www.evidenceincamera.co.uk/ (Aerial Reconnaissance archive of photographs)

SCOTTISH MILITARY RESEARCH

http://www.scotlandspeople.gov.uk/content/help/index.aspx?965 (Scottish Military research tips and links)

http://www.btinternet.com/~james.mckay/dispatch.htm (Scottish Military history society)

AUSTRALIAN FORCES

http://members.ozemail.com.au/~clday/WWI.htm (WWI Australian soldiers born in India)

http://members.iinet.net.au/~perthdps/military/links.htm#General (Military links from an Australian perspective)

CANADIAN FORCES

http://www.rootsweb.com/~canmil/index.html (Military history in Canada)

US FORCES & WARS

http://home.att.net/~wee-monster/military.html (Links to US Military resources)
http://www.excite.co.uk/directory/Society/Genealogy/Military (Mostly US military links)
http://www.militaryindexes.com/civilwar/ (US Civil War links and resources)
http://genrootsblog.blogspot.com/2006/07/civil-war-pension-service-records-tips.html (Aid to finding US Civil War pension and service records)
http://www.fylde.demon.co.uk/welcome.htm#CONTENTS (Australian website with links to Vietnam War pages)

AFGHANISTAN CONFLICTS

http://members.tripod.com/%7EGlosters/FAfghan.htm (Officers killed in the Victorian Afghan conflict 1838-1842)
http://members.tripod.com/%7EGlosters/afghStaf.htm (Officers killed 1878-1880, with photographs)
http://members.tripod.com/%7EGlosters/afghcav.htm (Cavalry men killed 1878-1880, with photographs)
http://members.tripod.com/%7EGlosters/afghinf.htm (Infantry officers killed 1878-1880, with photographs)
http://www.garenewing.co.uk/angloafghanwar/waroffice/regiments.php (Regiments involved in the Anglo-Afghan wars 1878-1880)
http://members.tripod.com/%7EGlosters/guides.htm (List of those killed at the Kabul massacre, with photographs 1879)
http://www.redcoat.info/iraq2003.htm (Officers killed in the Afghan conflict 2004-2007)
http://members.tripod.com/%7EGlosters/iraq2003.htm (Officers killed 2004-2007)

AFRICA including BOER & ZULU WARS

http://southafricawargraves.org/ (Site of the South African War Graves Project with links, searches and international list of countries with South African war graves)
http://www.wartimesindex.co.uk/infopage.php?menu=wars&display=1stBoer (Background to 1st Boer War 1880-1881)
http://www.wartimesindex.co.uk/infopage.php?menu=wars&display=2ndBoer (Background to 2nd Boer War 1899-1902)
http://www.genuki.org.uk/big/eng/YKS/Misc/Transcriptions/WRY/LeedsTownHallBoerWarPlaque.html (Men who served in the Boer War, from a Leeds plaque)
http://www.genuki.org.uk/big/eng/DUR/GatesheadWarDead/BoerMemorial.html (Gateshead Boer War casualties)
http://genuki.cs.ncl.ac.uk/DEV/Exeter/WarMemorial.html (Boer War volunteers' memorial list – Exeter)
http://met.open.ac.uk/genuki/big/eng/bkm/Military/Boer_War/Latimer/ (Name list from Boer War memorial, Latimer, Bucks)

http://members.tripod.com/%7EGlosters/south.htm (British officers killed in South Africa 1878-1879, with photographs)

http://www.redcoat.info/sasdlx1.htm (Lists of soldiers killed 1877-1879 from many regiments including Natal mounted police)

http://www.wartimesindex.co.uk/infopage.php?menu=wars&display=Ashanti (Background to British involvement in the Ashanti Wars 1873-1900)

http://members.tripod.com/%7EGlosters/Rhodesia96.htm (British officers killed in Rhodesia 1896)

http://members.tripod.com/%7EGlosters/africa5.htm (Officers and Royal Marines killed in Africa 1852-1908)

http://members.tripod.com/%7EGlosters/somali.htm (Officers killed in Somaliland 1901-1904)

http://www.wartimesindex.co.uk/infopage.php?menu=wars&display=Zulu (Background to British involvement in the Zulu War, 1879)

ASIA (GENERAL)

http://www.indiaman.com/regiments.htm (Information regarding British regiments who served in Asia)

http://www.movinghere.org.uk/galleries/roots/asian/servicerecords/servicerecords. htm (Information on finding records of servicemen recruited in Asia)

BORNEO

http://www.roll-of-honour.org.uk/atrocities/sandakan/html/roll.htm (Database of British nationals who died as Japanese POWs at Sandarac, North Borneo)

BURMA

http://members.tripod.com/%7EGlosters/burmamem1.htm (Officers killed in the Burma conflicts 1824- 1930)

http://members.tripod.com/%7EGlosters/IP1.htm (India and Burma British Police killed 1888-1942)

CHINA

http://www.wartimesindex.co.uk/infopage.php?menu=wars&display=China (Background to the British involvement in the Chinese Opium Wars 1839-1860)

http://members.tripod.com/%7EGlosters/china60.htm (British Officers who died in China 1842-1901)

http://www.wartimesindex.co.uk/infopage.php?menu=wars&display=BoxerRebellion (Background to Boxer Rebellion in China 1900)

CIVIL WAR IN ENGLAND

http://www.british-history.ac.uk/search.asp?query1=civil+war (Official documents referring to the Civil War period)

CRIMEAN WAR

http://www.british-genealogy.com/forums/forumdisplay.php?f=311 (Crimean War forum)
http://www.wartimesindex.co.uk/infopage.php?menu=wars&display=Crimea (Background to the Crimea War 1854-1856)

EGYPT 1882-1885 & SUDAN 1896-1897

http://members.tripod.com/%7EGlosters/egyptz.htm (List of Officers killed, with some photographs)
http://www.redcoat.info/egyptroll82.htm (Soldiers killed in Egypt 1882-1885)
http://www.wartimesindex.co.uk/infopage.php?menu=wars&display=EgyptAndSudan (Background to the Victorian conflict in the Sudan 1882)

FALKLANDS WAR 1982

http://www.raf.mod.uk/falklands/rollofhonour.html (Roll of honour of all servicemen who fought this war)
http://members.tripod.com/%7EGlosters/falkland.htm (Army Officers killed in 1982 - includes those from other services also)

INDIAN CONFLICTS

http://members.tripod.com/%7EGlosters/memindex3.htm (List of those who died during the Indian Mutiny plus lots of other campaigns)
http://members.tripod.com/%7EGlosters/punniar.htm (Officers killed at Punniar and Maharajpore, India 1843)
http://members.tripod.com/%7EGlosters/Mudki.htm (Officers who died at Battle of Mudki, 1845)
http://members.tripod.com/%7EGlosters/Feroz.htm (Officers who died at Battle of Ferozsha, 1845)
http://members.tripod.com/%7EGlosters/Aliwal.htm (Officers who died in Battles of Badhowal, Aliwal and Sobraon, 1846)
http://www.redcoat.info/sutsl1.htm (Sutlej Campaign casualties listed alphabetically)
http://members.tripod.com/%7EGlosters/murder48.htm (British representatives murdered at Punjab, sparking the Punjab campaign)
http://members.tripod.com/%7EGlosters/Multan.htm (Officers who died at the siege of Multan, 1848-1849)
http://members.tripod.com/%7EGlosters/Chili.htm (British Officers 1849 who died at Battle of Chillianwala and Heights of Dullah, plus native officers)

http://members.tripod.com/%7EGlosters/Gujerat.htm (Officers who died at Battle of Gujerat, 1849)
http://members.tripod.com/%7EGlosters/Ramnag.htm (Officers who died at Ramnagur, 1848)
http://members.tripod.com/%7EGlosters/Exped.htm (Indians who died in the various Indian Expeditions, 1850-1888 – including Persia [Iran] and Bhutan)
http://members.tripod.com/%7EGlosters/india1908.htm (Officers killed in India 1908-1947)

IRAQ

http://www.redcoat.info/iraq2003.htm (List of Officers killed in Afghanistan and Iraq conflicts 2003-2007)

IRELAND

http://members.tripod.com/%7EGlosters/Ireland16.htm (British Officers and RUC officers killed in Irish Rebellion 1916)
http://members.tripod.com/%7EGlosters/ulster6999.htm (Officers killed in Northern Ireland 1969-1999)

JACOBITE & WILLIAMITE CONFLICTS

http://en.wikipedia.org/wiki/Williamite_war_in_Ireland (Jacobite War in Ireland)
http://www.british-history.ac.uk/search.asp?query1=jacobites (Online resources and document transcriptions)
http://www.alanwills.co.uk/ (Comprehensive Jacobite references, links and resources)
http://www.regiments.org/wars/17thcent/89stuart.htm (Jacobite War website 1689-1692)
http://www.nationalarchives.gov.uk/catalogue/Leaflets/ri2128.htm (National Archives' fact sheet - records held regarding Jacobite Risings of 1715 and 1745)
http://www.highlanderweb.co.uk/culloden/jacobite.htm (Timeline of the Jacobite Rebellion)
http://www.northumbrianjacobites.org.uk/ (Northumbrian Jacobites home page)
http://www.nas.gov.uk/guides/military.asp (Guide to Jacobite and other military records in Scottish National Archives)
http://www.rls.org.uk/database/record.php?usi=000-000-001-458-L (Illustrated study pack of Jacobite Rebellion 1745 and Culloden)
http://users.tinyonline.co.uk/amchardy/McHardy/Jacobites.htm (McHardy site with names of Jacobites)
http://www.foda.org.uk/oaths/intro/introduction4.htm (Names of Jacobite supporters in Devon)
http://lists.rootsweb.com/index/intl/SCT/JACOBITES.html (Jacobite genealogy mailing list)

JAVA REGION

http://www.roll-of-honour.org.uk/atrocities/600%5FGunners%5FParty/index.htm
(Database of British prisoners and survivors of the 600 Gunners Party)
http://members.tripod.com/%7EGlosters/java.htm (Officers killed at Java, Isle of
France, Mauritius 1810-1813)

KOREA

http://www.archives.gov/research/korean-war/ (Links to Korean War websites
including casualties)
http://www.militaryindexes.com/koreanwar/index.html (Online Korean War resources)
http://members.tripod.com/%7EGlosters/koreaomem1.htm (British officers killed
1950-1953)

KOSOVO

http://members.tripod.com/%7EGlosters/falkland.htm (Short list of officers killed
1999-2004 – scroll to bottom of Falklands page)

MALAYA 1948-1962

http://members.tripod.com/%7EGlosters/malaya.htm (List of officers killed)

MALAYSIA / MALLACA

http://members.tripod.com/%7EGlosters/malacca31.htm (Short list of officers killed in
Mallaca)
http://members.tripod.com/%7EGlosters/perak.htm (Officers/men at Perak, 1876-77)

MALTA

http://www.maltafamilyhistory.com/ (British Forces family history connections in Malta)

MAORI WARS / NEW ZEALAND WARS

http://www.wartimesindex.co.uk/infopage.php?menu=wars&display=NewZealand
(Background to British involvement in the Maori wars 1844-1865)
http://www.redcoat.info/nzwar.htm (Officers who died during the conflicts 1844-1864)
http://www.redcoat.info/nzwar1.htm (Soldiers and navy personnel 1845-1864)

NAPOLEONIC WARS

http://www.napoleonguide.com/battle_trafalgar.htm (Outline of battle of Trafalgar with
Napoleonic links)

http://www.genuki.org.uk/big/eng/Trafalgar/ (Names of ships, officers and men who fought at Trafalgar on 21st October 1805)
http://www.nationalarchives.gov.uk/trafalgarancestors/ (Search for men who fought at the battle of Trafalgar)
http://www.napoleon-series.org/military/organization/c_spanish.html (Spanish recruits in the British Army 1812-1813)
http://members.tripod.com/%7EGlosters/allwat.htm (Peninsular /Waterloo veterans 1800s)
http://members.tripod.com/%7EGlosters/QB1.htm (Quatre-Bras officers and regiments 1815)
http://www.old-liverpool.co.uk/Waterloo.html (Lancashire men in Battle of Waterloo)
http://www.genuki.org.uk/big/Helena.html (List of those on the Island of St Helena during Napoleon's detention there 1815-1821)

SEVEN YEARS WAR (1756-1763)

http://www.historyofwar.org/articles/wars_sevenyears.html (A site dedicated to the Seven Years War)

WAR OF 1812

http://www.warof1812.ca/1812link.htm (Links and information regarding British involvement)
http://www.carolyar.com/1812.htm (Website dedicated to the 1812 war between Britain and America)

WORLD WAR I

http://www.iwm.org.uk/ (Imperial War Museum site)
http://www.cwgc.org/somme/ (Battle of the Somme – day by day account with detailed maps and photograph gallery)
http://www.1914-1918.net/regular.htm (Links regarding regular soldiers in WWI)
http://www.1914-1918.net/kitchen.htm (All about Kitchener's Men or the 'New Armies')
http://www.slaidburn.org.uk/roll_of_honour_1.htm (Slaidburn, Yorkshire Roll of Honour of servicemen who lost their lives in WWI)
http://www.ewhurstfallen.co.uk/Roll%20of%20Honour.htm (A list of those who died in WWI from Ewhurst and Ellen's Green, Surrey.
http://www.barton-under-needwood.org.uk/rolhon.html (WWI and WWII war dead lists from Barton under Needwood, Staffs.)
http://www.genuki.org.uk/search/ (Type the words 'roll of honour' into this search engine to find nearly a thousand lists of war dead and similar web pages throughout Britain and Ireland)
http://www.hellotommy.co.uk/Great_War_Links/great_war_links.html (A good selection of WWI links)

http://www.hertfordshire-genealogy.co.uk/data/occupations/military-ww1.htm (Various links regarding WWI in Hertfordshire)
http://www.worldwar1.com/tsearch.htm (Search facility for WWI information)
http://net.lib.byu.edu/~rdh7/wwi/ (WWI document archive)
http://www.fylde.demon.co.uk/welcome.htm#CONTENTS (Hellfire Corner – stories and anecdotes from WWI)
http://www.1914-1918.net/grandad/avl.html (A page with links to some online Absent Voters Lists throughout the country)

WORLD WAR II

http://www.iwm.org.uk/ (Imperial War Museum site)
http://www.secondworldwar.co.uk/links.html (Page with some unusual WWII links)
http://www.britain-at-war.org.uk/html/links.htm (Britain at War - links to records and resources)
http://www.ers.cqm.co.uk/rservice/wwlk.htm (Scottish WWII links)
http://www.wartimememories.co.uk/links.html (Wartime Memories Project page with lots of useful links)
http://www.primaryresources.co.uk/history/history1.htm (Primary resources website with some unusual links)
http://www.ibiblio.org/pha/ (List of links to World War II resources)
http://www.btp.police.uk/History%20Society/Publications/History%20Society/Roll%20of%20honor/Printable/WW2%20Printable.htm (WWII roll of honour for British Transport Police)
http://www.war-experience.org/index.html (Second World War Experience Centre resources page)
http://www.besthistorysites.net/WWII.shtml (World War II from a US perspective)
http://www.ww2poster.co.uk/ (Site concentrating on World War II posters)
http://www.csi.ad.jp/ABOMB/index.html (The Atom Bomb Museum website)
http://www.roll-of-honour.com/Regiments/ (Rolls of honour by regiment with search facilities)
http://www.24hourmuseum.org.uk/nwh_gfx_en/ART44213.html (Details of plans for the release of servicemen's records on the net)
http://www.bbc.co.uk/history/worldwars/wwtwo/ (BBC site about WWII, with links)
http://www.codesandciphers.org.uk/ (Details about the use of codes in WWII and those involved)
http://www.gazettes-online.co.uk/ww2.asp?webType=0 (*London Gazette* WWII archive – search facility)
http://www.cyber-heritage.co.uk/cutaway/ (Site dedicated to WWII images)
http://www.worldwar-2.net/ (WWII timeline)

PRISONERS OF WAR & INTERNEES

http://www.historylearningsite.co.uk/british_internees.htm (Resources regarding interned British civilians living in Germany during WWII)

http://user.itl.net/~glen/CivilianInternees.html (Page about Japanese civilian internees in Singapore during World War II)

http://www.isle-of-man.com/manxnotebook/famhist/genealgy/intern.htm (Internment camps in the Isle of Man)

http://user.itl.net/~glen/asianintro.html (POWs and civilian prisoners in Asia)

http://www.historylearningsite.co.uk/british_pow.htm (British POWs in Germany)

http://www.nationalarchives.gov.uk/documentsonline/pow.asp (National Archives' resources)

http://www.nationalarchives.gov.uk/catalogue/RdLeaflet.asp?sLeafletID=7 (National Archives records leaflet for researchers)

http://www.petrowilliamus.co.uk/murals/murals.htm (Site dedicated to the murals painted by POWs in Changi camp)

http://www.historylearningsite.co.uk/changi_pow_camp.htm (Another Changi POW site)

http://home.comcast.net/~winjerd/POWCamp1.htm (An insight into life and death at a POW camp in war-time Japan)

http://www.historylearningsite.co.uk/german_pow.htm (Site about German POWs)

http://worldwar2database.com/html/japanpow.htm (Japanese POWs in Allied hands – resources and search facilities)

http://www.historylearningsite.co.uk/colditz.htm (Colditz POW camp resource page)

http://www.powtaiwan.org/men.html (Taiwan POWs database with search facility)

http://www.movinghere.org.uk/galleries/roots/asian/pullingittogether/pows.htm (Asiatic Merchant seamen POWs information)

RED CROSS / RED CRESCENT WORKERS

http://www.historylearningsite.co.uk/red_cross_and_world_war_two.htm (Details of the work of the Red Cross in WWII)

http://www.redcross.org.uk/standard.asp?id=2623&cachefixer (British Red Cross Museum and Archives with links to WWI and WWII workers)

http://www.redcross.int/en/history/archive.asp (Access to International Red Cross / Red Crescent archives)

http://www.redcross.org.uk/standard.asp?id=3008&cachefixer (Red Cross site with information for researchers)

CONSCIENTIOUS OBJECTORS TO MILITARY SERVICE

http://www.nationalarchives.gov.uk/catalogue/RdLeaflet.asp?sLeafletID=25 (National Archives' guide to tracing conscientious objectors and those exempt from service)

EVACUEES

http://www.extra.rdg.ac.uk/evacueesarchive/ (Research Centre for Evacuee and War Child Studies)

http://clutch.open.ac.uk/schools/standrews00/evac_nthbucks.htm (Information about evacuation in Buckinghamshire)

http://www.emsource.org.uk/templates/temp_ems_items.rm?id=442&topic=0&from =97&num=16 (Links to evacuee resources)

http://www.war-experience.org/education/evacuation/evacuation-intro.asp (Background to the evacuee plans plus link to personal stories)

http://www.bbc.co.uk/history/ww2children/letters/letters_intro.shtml (Extracts from evacuees letters)

http://www.woodlands-junior.kent.sch.uk/Homework/war/evacuation.htm (Educational resource concerning evacuees)

WAR BRIDES

http://www.geocities.com/Heartland/Meadows/9710/WarBrides.html (Site dedicated to US war brides with lots of interesting genealogy add-ons)

http://www.passengerlists.co.uk/search.htm (Search war brides on passenger ships)

http://www.canadianwarbrides.com/passenger-lists.asp (War brides bound for Canada)

WOMEN AT WAR

http://www.nationalarchives.gov.uk/catalogue/RdLeaflet.asp?sLeafletID=142 (National Archives' resources)

http://www.nationalarchives.gov.uk/documentsonline/waac.asp (Women's Army Auxiliary Corps records at The National Archives)

http://www.nationalarchives.gov.uk/catalogue/Leaflets/ri2287.htm (Online information leaflet for tracing WRAF, WAAC, WRNS and other female war records)

http://www.btinternet.com/~prosearch/tomspage9.html ('Women's Services during the Great War' - website with information and links including nursing services)

http://www.familyrecords.gov.uk/focuson/womeninuniform/default.htm (Women in Uniform: information and links including army nursing)

http://www.users.zetnet.co.uk/dms/past/ww1/women.html (Photographs of women in the services WWI)

http://www.spartacus.schoolnet.co.uk/FWWwomen.htm (Links to biographies of women at all levels during WWI)

http://www.oucs.ox.ac.uk/ltg/projects/jtap/tutorials/intro/women/ (Wartime poetry from women involved in WWI)

http://www.1914-1918.net/women.htm (WWI links to women at war in various organisations)

http://freepages.history.rootsweb.com/~garter1/women.htm (Women recorded as serving with British regiments)

http://www.scarletfinders.co.uk/ (Military nursing website)
http://www.archiveshub.ac.uk/news/0411wla.html (Finding aids and references to Women's Land Army records)
http://www.wartimememories.co.uk/womenslandarmy.html (Information, memories and photographs about the Women's Land Army)
http://www.spartacus.schoolnet.co.uk/2WWlandarmy.htm (General website about Women's Land Army)
http://www.stephen-stratford.co.uk/women_gcs.htm (Women holders of the George Cross)
http://www.cyber-heritage.co.uk/ww2women/ (Portrayals of women in WWII advertising)
http://www.nmm.ac.uk/server/show/conMediaFile.3162 (Pictures of WWII uniforms for women with links to other resources)

PENSION & SERVICE RECORDS (ALL SERVICES)

http://www.nationalarchives.gov.uk/news/stories/150.htm (National Archives' WWI pension records with link to online search)
http://www.archives.gov/research/order/vets-records.html (Access to Military Service and Pensions information)
http://www.nationalarchives.gov.uk/pathways/firstworldwar/service_records/sr_soldiers.htm (Guide and links for all services pensions)
http://www.movinghere.org.uk/galleries/roots/jewish/service/service.htm (Jewish service records)
http://www.24hourmuseum.org.uk/nwh_gfx_en/ART44213.html (Accessing WWII pension records online)
http://www.1914-1918.net/grandad/grandad_records.html (Illustration of an army service record with tips on how to obtain them for various regiments)
http://www.royal-navy.mod.uk/server/show/nav.00h007001 (How to obtain Navy service records)

MEDALS

http://www.nationalarchives.gov.uk/familyhistory/guide/army/medalrolls.htm (National Archives' guide to medal records – search WWI medal rolls online)
http://www.nationalarchives.gov.uk/documentsonline/help/Abbreviations-rank.asp (Abbreviations found on WWI medal cards)
http://www.royal-navy.mod.uk/server/show/nav.00h007001 (How to obtain Navy medals)
http://www.worldmedals.co.uk/Rib/Britrib/britribb.htm (Illustrated British medals list – commercial site)
http://www.mod.uk/DefenceInternet/ContactUs/MedalsEnquiries.htm (Enquiry form for Army, Navy or Air Force medals)

http://www.victoriacrosssociety.com/links.htm (Victoria Cross Society website with links for researchers)

http://www.gc-database.co.uk/biblio.htm (George Cross database of resources)

http://www.medals.org.uk/ (Searchable Medals of the World website)

http://www.royalhumanesociety.org.uk/awards/winners/home.htm (List of medal and award winners from Royal Humane Society)

http://www.1914-1918.net/grandad/grandad_medals.html (Research involving WWI medals)

http://www.burmastar.org.uk/military_history1.htm (Burma Star military history links)

http://www.stephen-stratford.co.uk/wwii_medals.htm (All about WWII medals – illustrated)

WAR GRAVES & MEMORIALS

http://www.cwgc.org/ (Commonwealth War Graves Commission site – free search for graves and memorials online, also civilian roll of honour)

http://www.britishwargraves.org.uk/searching_for_a_grave.asp (Search for a war grave/memorial)

http://www.ukniwm.org.uk/ (Search the National Inventory of War Graves)

http://www.wartimememories.co.uk/information.html (International war graves links)

http://www.warmemorials.org/Website/About/About.htm (Website of War Memorials Trust, formerly known as the Friends of War Memorials)

http://www.essex.police.uk/memorial/ww1.htm (Essex Police Memorial Trust website)

http://www.roll-of-honour.com/ (War memorials throughout the country plus supplementary war information)

http://www.oldukphotos.com/ (Photographs of memorials in Britain and overseas)

http://www.genuki.org.uk/big/eng/Indexes/NE_WarDead/Abbreviations.html (Abbreviations found on rolls of honour and war memorials)

http://www.angelfire.com/mp/memorials/memindz1.htm (Website collecting British military memorial lists for all wars and campaigns throughout the world)

http://members.tripod.com/%7EGlosters/guards1.htm (Guards Officers memorial inscriptions – Wellington Barracks, early conflicts1665-1881)

http://www.genuki.org.uk/big/eng/Indexes/NE_WarDead/ (List of WWII civilians killed by enemy action in Northumberland, Durham and Yorkshire)

WEBRINGS

Webrings are sites that link various other similar subject sites to each other. Many of them are run by individuals. There are a number of groups of genealogy sites like this and you can join any ring or even start your own.

http://dir.yahoo.com/Arts/Humanities/History/Genealogy/ (Start your own genealogy webring here)

http://k.webring.com/hub?ring=ukgen (List of sites in the UK Genealogy webring)
http://dir.webring.com/rw?d=Family___Home/Genealogy/ (View rings, forums or create a ring)
http://www.accessgenealogy.com/rings/ (US-based webring for genealogists)

WILLS, ADMINISTRATION & PROBATE

Wills, administration and probate records are invaluable to family history research because they give us details of names, relationships, locations of property and land. In addition they provide insights into the lifestyle of our ancestors. Strictly, a will contains the actual instructions given by a person as to what should be done about his or her affairs after death, whilst a *testament* referred to the distribution of his or her property. *Inventories* of the deceased person's possessions often accompany old wills and testaments. The distinction between these documents has been blurred in modern times and many aspects are combined in a modern will. *Probate* is the legal process of settling the estate of a deceased person by officially resolving all claims and sanctioning the distribution of the property. All wills and *administrations* (often referred to as 'admons' and issued if there was no will) proven in England and Wales after 1858 are held in the Principal Registry of the Family Division in Holborn. Holdings are indexed alphabetically by surname and year and the entries contain valuable name, address and occupational details. Before 1858 wills were proved in a multitude of local Church courts. Death Duty Registers record wills and bequests for estates liable to death duties.

http://www.genuki.org.uk/big/eng/Probate.html (County by county guide to English probate record sources)
http://nationalarchives.gov.uk/documentsonline/wills.asp (Search wills proved at the Prerogative Court of Canterbury 1384-1858 online)
http://www.ancestry.co.uk/search/rectype/vital/epr/main.aspx (Search parish and probate records)
http://www.york.ac.uk/inst/bihr/guideleaflets/ProbateRecords_wheretofind.pdf (A simple guide to finding probate records)
http://www.nationalarchives.gov.uk/catalogue/RdLeaflet.asp?sLeafletID=168&j=1 (National Archives' guide to probate records)
http://www.bl.uk/collections/oiocfamilyhistory/familywills.html (British library holdings)
http://www.ukdocuments.com/wills.php?gclid=CNm_tZvvzowCFQbmlAod50kPrg (Commercial site offering to search official probate indexes from 11th January 1858 onwards)
http://www.hmcourts-service.gov.uk/cms/1226.htm (Government site with a guide to obtaining copies of probate records)
http://www.ukgenealogy.co.uk/favorites/wills-probate.html (Search here for British and Irish probate records, 1500s to 1800s)
http://www.medievalgenealogy.org.uk/sources/probate.shtml (Site with links to medieval probate records and resources throughout Britain)

http://www.wills4all.netfirms.com/names_in_wills.htm (Growing list of names found in wills throughout Britain)

http://west-penwith.org.uk/probate/index.htm (West Penwith probate records online)

http://www.wirksworth.org.uk/B60-WBRA.htm (Some Derbyshire probates 1535-1800)

http://www.gmcro.co.uk/family_history/wills.htm (Greater Manchester County Record site regarding probate indexes with links to other area probate registries)

http://www.northamptonshire.gov.uk/Community/record/probate.htm (How to access Northamptonshire probate records)

http://webs.lanset.com/azazella/probate_supp.html (Selection of Cornish probate records)

http://www.canterhill.co.uk/davideastkent/kpr1.htm (Practical guide to Kent probate records)

http://archives.norfolk.gov.uk/guide/nroprob.htm (Guide to Norfolk probate record holdings)

http://www.wirksworth.org.uk/WILLS.htm (Derbyshire wills)

http://www.wirksworth.org.uk/WAdX1.htm#A (Derbyshire administrations list)

http://www.scottishdocuments.com/wills.asp (Scottish digitisation project for wills and other historic documents)

DEATH DUTY REGISTERS

http://www.nationalarchives.gov.uk/documentsonline/death-duty.asp (Search death duty registers 1796-1811 online at The National Archives)

http://www.familyrecords.gov.uk/frc/research/deathdutymain.htm (Illustrated guide with links)

family history on the net

Index